PENGUIN BOOKS

DRUGS, ALCOHOL, AND YOUR CHILDREN

Judith S. Seixas, a credentialed alcoholism counselor, has written many books for young readers, including *Alcohol: What It Is, What It Does*; *Drugs: What They Are, What They Do*; and *Living with a Parent Who Drinks Too Much*. She lives in Hastings-on-Hudson, New York.

Geraldine Youcha is the author of *Minding the Children: Child Care in America from Colonial Times to the Present* and *Women and Alcohol: A Dangerous Pleasure*. She has written frequently about drug use and its side effects on the family for major magazines. She lives in New City, New York.

Judith Seixas and Geraldine Youcha are the coauthors of *Children of Alcoholism: A Survivor's Manual*.

Drugs,
Alcohol,
and Your
Children

What Every Parent Needs to Know

Judith S. Seixas

Geraldine Youcha

 PENGUIN BOOKS

PENGUIN BOOKS
Published by the Penguin Group
Penguin Putnam Inc., 375 Hudson Street,
New York, New York 10014, U.S.A.
Penguin Books Ltd, 27 Wrights Lane,
London W8 5TZ, England
Penguin Books Australia Ltd, Ringwood,
Victoria, Australia
Penguin Books Canada Ltd, 10 Alcorn Avenue,
Toronto, Ontario, Canada M4V 3B2
Penguin Books (N.Z.) Ltd, 182–190 Wairau Road,
Auckland 10, New Zealand

Penguin Books Ltd, Registered Offices:
Harmondsworth, Middlesex, England

First published in the United States of America by
Crown Publishers, Inc., 1989
This revised and updated edition published in Penguin Books 1999

10 9 8 7 6 5 4 3 2 1

LIBRARY OF CONGRESS CATALOGING-IN-PUBLICATION DATA
Seixas, Judith S.
    Drugs, alcohol, and your children : what every parent needs to
know / Judith S. Seixas, Geraldine Youcha.
        p.   cm.
    ISBN 0 14 02.8047 2
    1. Youth—Alcohol use—United States.   2. Alcoholism—United
States—Prevention.   3. Youth—Drug use—United States.   4. Drug
abuse—United States—Prevention.   5. Parenting—United States.
I. Youcha, Geraldine.   II. Title.
HV5135.S45   1999
649'.4—dc21   99–20614

Printed in the United States of America
Set in Garamond
Designed by Patrice Sheridan

For
Sara, Lisa, Naomi, Rachel, Mikaela,
Eli, Gustav, Isabel, Emma, and Zachary

Preface

Since this book was first published ten years ago, enormous changes have swept the world of drug use and abuse by young people. An epidemic that seemed to be burning out has been rekindled, and although it has not reached the peak levels of the late 1970s and may even have started a slow decline, children caught in its blaze now start using drugs earlier than ever. New drugs are more dangerous; old drugs are stronger than before, and more likely to be contaminated with other toxic substances. AIDS has made drug use—and the early and unprotected sexual activity often associated with it—a death threat.

With a new sense of urgency, governments, from local to national, are getting involved in keeping youngsters from starting to smoke, and from taking the first steps toward the use of other drugs. A five-year, one-billion-dollar federal advertising campaign aimed at prevention is targeting children ten years old and younger, a belated recognition that if you don't catch them early, you may not catch them at all. Tobacco has finally been widely recognized as an addictive drug, and the surgeon general calls smoking "the most preventable cause of death in America."

Yet many things have not changed. Parents still feel helpless, bewildered, and afraid. They still deny what they see, and children are still tempted to use alcohol, tobacco, and other drugs as part of the ritual of growing up. Marijuana remains the illegal drug of choice, and alcohol the favorite social lubricant. With both the persistent patterns and the new dangers in mind, we have revised, expanded, and updated this book to serve as a guide for today's concerned parents.

Judith S. Seixas
Geraldine Youcha
January 1999

Acknowledgments

We would like to thank our editors past and present, Pamela Thomas, Erica Marcus, and Caroline White, for their patience and perceptive comments; Liz Darhansoff, our agent, for her continuing faith in us; Jan Lurie for her invaluable editorial advice; Sara Rab for her expert research assistance; Professor Stacy Caplow for her careful reading of part of the manuscript; Eileen Browning and Ellen Morehouse for their help and support; the parents and children who told us their stories; and all those who work with young people and their families and took the time to guide us. We also thank our loved ones for their astute suggestions and encouragement.

Contents

Introduction

A friend told us recently that his son is in prison for drug-dealing. That was not the last thing we expected to hear, but it was close to it. Our friend, a successful lawyer, said that he and his wife were devastated when they discovered that their son had been picked up and would be brought to trial. Their younger children were ordinary, untroubled, average kids, but now the parents were concerned about them, too. How did they know that they wouldn't end up as their brother had—in jail? These parents had little forewarning and they had not realized the severity of the problem until it was too late.

There are millions of parents like our friend. They have tried their best, but have ended up with a drug-related problem or tragedy on their hands. They may have discovered a child smoking marijuana or sniffing glue; or they may be contending with a child who is drug-addicted or suffering the consequences of early and repeated drug use. Or, in the worst possible scenario, they may have lost a child who has killed himself with an overdose or has ended up in a fatal alcohol-related automobile crash.

Is there anything that can be done to prevent these catastrophes? Is there anything parents going through tumultuous times can learn that may, in any way at all, lighten the burden or change the course of events? How can parents help their children before the trouble begins? What should they do when they realize something is askew? To whom can they turn? What should they know about chemical dependency and the power of mind-altering drugs? How can extended families and friends unite when there is trouble? When does a child need help? When should it be withheld? Where can help be found? And what does help really mean? Can parents make a difference, or is it mostly a matter of luck? Our task in this book is to address these questions.

The answers do not come easily. They are incomplete and they are different for different people, so the best we can do is present guidelines and suggestions. You must choose what you need for yourself, your family, and any child of yours who has stepped off solid ground into troubled waters.

When our own children were adolescents in the sixties and seventies we were naive about drug use. "Hippie" was a new word in our vocabulary. We didn't recognize those serrated leaves that grew so abundantly in the window boxes and flowerpots on dormitory windowsills. We were stunned when many of our children's contemporaries ended up in handcuffs for possessing marijuana. Some young people had temporary drug-induced psychoses, and others had disastrous drug trips that permanently wrecked their minds. When Woody Allen sneezed away thousands of dollars' worth of cocaine in *Annie Hall* and the young audience laughed, many of us didn't get the joke. We didn't realize what he was sneezing away, or what, for that matter, was so funny.

Today's parents, too, are woefully naive and baffled, even if they themselves survived the drug-using sixties. These times are harrowing ones. The drug scene in America has changed dramatically; drugs are stronger, drug use is pervasive and more acceptable, and young people are using drugs at earlier and earlier ages. In the early nineties the drug epidemic that seemed to be subsiding somewhat came to disturbing new life. After five years of steady increases, marijuana use among eighth-graders was three times the earlier rate. High school seniors' use of hallucinogens, marijuana, and cocaine doubled. Today, although use seems to have leveled off or even declined slightly, particularly for younger adolescents, some figures remain nearly twice what they were in 1991.

Years ago when life seemed frightening or unfair, a teenager could either wait it out or fight back. Now there are easily available chemical remedies for the youngster who is confused and embarrassed by intense sexual feelings or scared about the future, for the boy who is unhappy because he is too short, for the girl who is in despair because she is flat-chested.

Adolescence is scary enough. It is a time when friends become as important as food, a time for trying new things—sometimes before the brain has caught up with the body. Teenagers have neither the experience nor the inclination to gauge probability, and often assume that if nothing bad happened the first time—whether it was driving fast, taking drugs, or having sex without protection—the chances of something awful happening later on lessen with each repetition of the act. They often vastly underestimate the risk of any dangerous activity, and feel themselves invulnerable.

When a middle-class eighteen-year-old girl was found dead in New York's Central Park, strangled during a sexual encounter by an underage drinking boyfriend after a visit to a neighborhood bar, her uncle reminded grieving friends and relatives at the funeral, "Anyone who has ever been eighteen years old knows that nothing bad can happen to you. That's the way it's supposed to be. Well, I guess we know now that it isn't true." The grim reality is that the annual death rate among adolescents in this country is still unacceptably high at about 98 per 100,000, even though it has gone down slightly since the 1980s. Drugs—including alcohol—and risk-taking are major contributors to the somber statistics.

To get some perspective on the problem we have talked to dozens of parents of troubled children. We have also interviewed scores of people whose daily lives and work put them in touch with teenagers and young adults. These include school personnel, the police, social workers, drug counselors, physicians, psychologists, and members of the clergy. They work in all parts of the country—New York City, Atlanta, Chicago, San Francisco, Los Angeles, and elsewhere. In addition, we have talked to young drug addicts and alcoholics, some of whom are recovering while others are still struggling to get well or have given up hope. (In telling their stories, we have used some real names and omitted or changed others.) For the sake of brevity and accuracy we have also often used the word "drug" to include alcohol, nicotine, and other drugs.

We certainly don't pretend to have answers to the complex personal and societal problems associated with chemical dependency. We do offer information and understanding to help parents untangle the knot they face day and night whether their children are four or fourteen or forty. Although research on alcohol, tobacco, and drug use and abuse is still in its early stages, it is accelerating. There may be substances that will reverse or neutralize the harm that already has been inflicted on the chemically dependent young; there may be greater understanding of why some children are more likely than others to engage in risk-taking behaviors; there may be advances in genetic engineering so that children who are predisposed to drug use can be treated to help them avoid the trap heredity has set. There is always a place for optimism.

PART 1

What to Look For

What's Really Happening

They'll swallow anything they think will help them to escape even if they don't know what it is. When a local pharmaceutical company dumped pills, they went and dug them up. Penicillin tablets were selling for three dollars each.

—A SUBURBAN LAW-ENFORCEMENT OFFICIAL

It is unrealistic to think your child can slide through adolescence without running into alcohol and other drugs, no matter where you live. Everything is available everywhere, with the average age of first use now hovering around twelve and continuing to drop. Every day more than three thousand children start smoking, and almost one-third of them will die later of tobacco-related illnesses. More than a million and a half heavy drinkers in this country are so

Most of the statistics in this chapter are based on the 1998 University of Michigan's Monitoring the Future study.

young they cannot buy liquor legally. Problem drinking is often associated with drug use, school problems, and teenage pregnancy, forming a devastating combination. The average age of first intercourse is sixteen, and each year one in ten teenage girls becomes pregnant. For the teenager who is sexually active or uses intravenous drugs, AIDS (acquired immunodeficiency syndrome) is an ever-present risk.

The world has changed. In 1963, four million people in this country had used an illegal drug at some time; by 1992, the figure was eighty million, close to one-third of the population. Today, almost half of all American teenagers have tried an illicit substance, usually marijuana, before graduating from high school. These are not necessarily the kids who "look funny," labeled by their schoolmates as "the druggies" or "the boozers." They are also the athletes, the successful students, and the class presidents, the good kids who just a few years ago were assumed to be immune. A New York State study of students in grades seven to twelve showed that, contrary to public expectation, it was in the affluent Hudson River suburbs and not New York City that the highest percentage of youngsters used drugs. Suburban kids in general use drugs at a rate higher than the national average. One counselor characterized this as "the better the income, the better the drug." In an alarming summary of what is happening today the Rev. Edward A. Malloy, president of Notre Dame University and head of a panel studying substance abuse in the 1990s, reported, "Never before have American adolescents been asked to grow up amid such a combustible and dangerous mix of substance abuse conditions—use and abuse by their peers, experimentation and abuse at younger ages, the widespread availability of all kinds of drugs to children and teens, the cultural glamorization of cigarettes, alcohol, and drugs, drug-infested public and private schools. Most disturbing is the fact that children are being exposed to these substances at younger and younger ages and are therefore more vulnerable to their tragic effects."

Teenagers think they know what they're using, but one of the most frightening realities of the drug scene is that what they get may not be what it appears to be. Pills sold as one drug are often another; pure drugs frequently are mixed with other dangerous substances. Forty percent of PCP users report that they first used the drug without knowing what they were taking. It is estimated that more than half the marijuana sold on the street is adulterated with substances such as PCP, heroin, or even embalming fluid. In addition, the marijuana of the 1990s is much stronger on average than that sold in the 1960s. (In the late sixties marijuana was 1 to 3 percent potent. In the nineties its potency can go as high as 15 percent.) Cocaine today is much purer—and cheaper—than ever before. "Crack" is the strongest, cheapest, and most quickly addictive form of the drug. Heroin, too, is purer and cheaper than ever, and can be smoked, snorted, and swallowed in capsules as well as injected. At "raves"—all-night, usually underground dancing parties—the wide range of psychedelics sold may be adulterated with a variety of other hazardous substances. The favorite, MDMA, known as Ecstasy, is often spiked with another drug.

Adolescent drug users risk death in other ways, too. Automobile accidents are the leading cause of death in this age group—and alcohol is implicated in almost half of these cases. Among youngsters fifteen to nineteen years old, suicide is the second leading cause of death, with nearly half the young people who take their own lives involved with alcohol or drugs. The tragic national statistic is that fourteen young people commit suicide every day. About 30 percent are drunk or high at the time, ten times more than thirty years ago. Guns are the most common suicide weapon. Equally disturbing is the fact that the number of children under the age of fifteen who killed themselves rose from forty in 1950 to more than three hundred in 1993. This is double the rate in the rest of the industrialized world. For a variety of reasons, life had become too much for them.

To give you some idea of the changed world children face today, here is a listing compiled by the Fullerton, California, police department and the California Department of Education of the top nonscholastic concerns in public schools in 1940 contrasted with a list based on a study by the National Center on Addiction and Substance Abuse at Columbia University in 1995:

Top Nonscholastic Concerns in Public Schools	
1940	1995
Talking	Drugs
Chewing gum	Social pressures (popu-
Making noise	larity)
Running in the halls	Crime and violence in
Getting out of turn in	school
line	Sexual issues (pregnancy,
Wearing improper clothing	abortion, disease)
Not putting paper in	Other crime and violence
wastebaskets	

HOW DID WE GET HERE?

Parents try to understand today's world through the world they experienced growing up. It won't work. The transition from simple disciplinary problems to major police and health problems is the result not only of the passage of time but of major social upheavals.

For one thing, divorce has become a way of life, placing extra burdens on single mothers. For another, mothers, divorced or not, are out of the house and in the workplace in great numbers alongside fathers.

We are also still living with the legacies of the sixties. These include:

- The Vietnam War and its residue of conscientious resistance to laws viewed as unfair
- The notion that parents and children should be friends and equals
- The social acceptability of drug use
- The idea that individual rights take precedence over social controls

As Dr. Mitchell Rosenthal, president of Phoenix House, a leading drug treatment center in New York, points out, "Too many Americans are torn between the urge to condemn behavior of which they disapprove and the need to tolerate what they have somehow come to believe is not a matter of their business."

Society no longer provides an automatic backup for a parent's prohibitions. There is no clear social message. There is not even a clear medical message. Earlier reports about marijuana and its dangers were ambiguous, but the

American Academy of Pediatrics now says, "The seriousness of the behavioral consequences of marijuana use is sufficient to cause great concern and prompt the pediatrician to counsel young people against any use of the drug." Marijuana was once thought to be nonaddictive, unlike other mood-altering drugs. James McBride, author of the best-selling book *The Color of Water*, remembers telling his friends when he was a pot-smoking teenager, " 'You can't get hooked on reefer . . . I can stop any time I want.' But deep inside I knew I was hooked." A study sponsored by the National Institute on Drug Abuse now confirms what he knew: Heavy marijuana smoking can lead to addiction, despite the fact that there are no abrupt withdrawal symptoms as there are with other drugs. Although this finding has been disputed, in 1996, marijuana was the number-one drug for almost two-thirds of the teenagers in treatment at the Pennsylvania-based Caron Foundation. Most authorities agree that for adolescents and preadolescents any marijuana smoking is hazardous. But youngsters focus on the conflicting reports and avoid looking at the latest information.

The messages regarding alcohol are also mixed. Parents may find themselves feeling uncomfortably out of step with the rest of the world if they say no. Many adults see beginning to drink as a rite of passage and moderate alcohol use as an integral part of their own lives.

The parents of some high school seniors in a New York suburb condoned a beer blast during school hours to celebrate the end of the year—and even bought the kegs for the party. Twenty students cut classes and drank at the home of one of them while the parents of that student were present. These parents, along with some others, were outraged when school officials suspended the students because classroom attendance was required—and alcohol illegal.

Parents such as these are ambivalent about alcohol use and fearful that taking a clear stand on drugs or alcohol will "destroy our relationship." One reason they won't risk alienating their children is that in these days of divorce, the child may reject one parent in favor of the other, more lenient one. Even when there are two parents at home, the family may have no other relatives nearby, so that children become inordinately important emotional props. Fearful of being rejected or deserted, some parents avoid taking firm or unpopular stands, and when parents abdicate, other structures act as substitutes. Cults, which offer firm rules, a father figure to admire and follow, and the certainties of community living, may owe some of their popularity to the uneasiness parents have about assuming these difficult, traditional "I'm the boss, you're the kid" roles. To be a good parent, Ellen Morehouse, executive director of Student Assistance Services, a New York–based alcohol and drug prevention organization, says firmly, "You have to love your kids enough to let them hate you."

A KID'S WORLD

As parents play an increasingly smaller role in their children's daily lives, a cohesive, powerful peer subculture that is recognized by both youngsters and society at large moves in to fill the void. Advertisers take advantage of this, enticing young people to use alcohol and tobacco, wear designer jeans, and join the hurry-up world of adults. Sixties music lyrics, still popular today, encourage drug-taking as a mind-expanding experience. Music videos provide graphic enactments of the drug-soaked lyrics of rock and rap. Movies and television build drugs and alcohol into the lives of the teenagers they show. The Internet, feared by parents as a purveyor of pornography, is also a source of information on the drug culture; a youngster can find out how to get high on LSD, grow marijuana, make "speed," snort cocaine, and exchange information with others in "chat rooms." Since trendiness is equated with popularity in the teenage world, drugs, smoking, and drinking are part of the picture.

The separate world that adolescents inhabit is often kept hidden from their parents. Puzzled parents say, "Where in the world do they get the stuff that they use? And where do they use it? I never see any of it around here."

The list of places where alcohol and drugs are used—often without adult awareness—reads like an atlas of the places teens gather: in cars—both parked and moving; in parking lots; in school hallways and stairs; in malls; outside the school lunchroom; in the woods. You might be startled to discover that on prom nights the elegant limousines that have become popular are really rolling bars, making it possible to extend the preprom cocktail parties that are condoned and sometimes provided by parents. At least, the thinking goes, they won't be driving after they've been drinking. Kids drink and smoke in their rooms, or in their friends' rooms, in homes when parents are away, and downstairs or upstairs when parents are present. "What do you think happens at those Friday night parties?" one teenager asked her naive parents. Tickets to rock concerts are seen as licenses to use drugs. Even church-related events, church schools, and camps are not immune.

The truth is that some kids will use whatever is afford-able and available, and they will use it anywhere they think they can get away with it. A seventeen-year-old boy just out of treatment for alcoholism says the second time he ever got drunk was at a drug-free school party. Some older boys he hardly knew drove by on their motorcycles with beer they had stolen, and he joined them in the woods "for five or six." Then he went back to the party and found he felt re-ally relaxed and was finally having a good time.

Like this boy, teenagers often get drugs and alcohol from their friends—either informally as a friendly gesture or for money. Kids—like their adult counterparts—say "dealer," not "pusher," and the dealer is often another youngster who deals on the side to pay the costs of his habit. It is a kind of condoned lawlessness, a two-way transaction that is not considered "bad" by either side.

The money used may come from allowances, or part-time jobs, or the sale of objects from home, or out of a parent's wallet. Although work has usually been seen as a good thing for a teenager, today's dangers present new problems. A re-cent study showed that young people who work twenty hours a week or more are more likely to smoke cigarettes, use drugs and alcohol, and have early sexual intercourse. J. Richard Udry of the University of North Carolina at Chapel Hill and a principal investigator of the study, suggests that working provides income "to get into trouble." Some youngsters re-port that their older coworkers supply them with drugs, and that parties with this new group of friends tend to include al-cohol and drugs. They often get these older friends to buy al-cohol for them. It's called "pimping beer."

Kids also get drugs and alcohol from their older sisters and brothers, and from their unwitting parents. A favorite supply depot is the family liquor cabinet. Before a junior high school dance, word went out that each child in a certain group was to bring an inch or two of liquor (not enough to be missed) to the school. These samples were pooled in a glass jar and the concoction was downed on the playground. A boy became drunk, then unconscious, and fell to the freezing ground. The dangerous game was discovered in time when someone ran to get adult help for him.

Being underage is not much of a deterrent. To get into bars, girls wear makeup and clothing that make them look older. Boys may wear jackets and even conservative hats. The false-ID market thrives, and word travels fast if a liquor store, supermarket, or bar is not too careful about "proofing" or "carding" for age. If youngsters are too young to try to fool a storekeeper, they hang around outside a liquor store and, as one teenager put it, "wait for a 'swinging dude' to go in. When he comes out we offer him money and he goes back in and buys us stuff, so even little kids can get their hands on liquor."

Drugs may even come out of the family medicine cabinet. A pharmacist regularly asks concerned parents, "Do you keep count of your pills?" Kids also buy mind-altering substances over the counter—computer cleaner (to sniff), glue, diet pills, nasal inhalers, vanilla extract, even cough medicine with a high alcohol content. They pass these around, share and share alike.

GRADE SCHOOL

One northern Virginia elementary school janitor found an unexpected bag of marijuana along with the expected candy wrappers when he cleaned the hallway. On the edge of another grade school's playground, junior high school students gather at lunchtime, smoke marijuana, and, in effect, entice the younger kids to join them. Grade-schoolers are well aware that some fifth- and sixth-graders smoke marijuana and cigarettes, drink alcohol, or sniff glue. Young children are even more likely than their older counterparts to use easily available household inhalants as mood changers. They sometimes get their first experience when they breathe in the innocuous helium from birthday balloons to make their voices sound funny. They may then start inhaling other substances that can kill brain cells.

A startling survey by *The Weekly Reader*, the national children's magazine, revealed that almost one-third of the fourth- to sixth-graders questioned felt that their classmates pressured them "a lot" to drink beer. The survey reports what children believe is happening, not necessarily what is really going on. But it is a reflection of their concern. They are both scared and fascinated. This report corroborates what many experts have pointed out: Prevention has to start long before the seventh grade.

JUNIOR HIGH SCHOOL

The peak time for starting smoking and drinking comes after grade school, in middle school or junior high. That is when nonusers become users and peer pressure gets stronger. Substance abuse of all kinds and the use of more than one drug at a time increase with grade level. Moreover, whatever else they use, they also use the drug their parents choose—alcohol. In 1998 one in seven eighth-graders reported drinking five or more drinks on one occasion during the previous two weeks.

When she was twelve years old, Terry went to a junior high school dance. She was pretty, popular, and the winner of the school essay contest. Her recently divorced mother went to a movie. When the mother got home she found a message from the school principal on her telephone answering machine: "Please call the school office immediately." At the junior high school, she found Terry in the girls' room, drunk and throwing up. Terry's mother remembers that as the principal talked to the parents of the preteens involved, "I sat there feeling like the last human being on Earth. I didn't have a clue as to what was going on." She discovered that Terry had been drinking the whole year—this wasn't the first incident. She went with the parents of six other youngsters to school the next week to discuss the problem. When they found out that their children were not members of the really troubled group—the "hard-core alcoholics in junior high school"—they were both relieved and horrified.

Alcohol is only one of the drugs kids start using regularly, once they leave grade school. The percentage of preteens reporting that they have friends using hard drugs more than doubled between 1996 and 1997.

HIGH SCHOOL

Almost half of all American teenagers try some illegal drug before the end of high school, and one in every seventeen high school seniors smokes marijuana daily. According to the University of Michigan's Monitoring the Future study, the figures for daily marijuana use are almost double the level of the late 1980s, but nowhere near the peak reached in 1979. Alcohol consumption, on the other hand, has stayed close to the same dismayingly high levels, with binge-drinking on a slow but steady increase until 1998, when it showed a slight decline. One in twenty-six high school seniors drinks daily and more than 31 percent have had five or more drinks on a single occasion within a two-week period. During the 1990s stimulants moved into fourth place on the popularity chart, after alcohol, tobacco, and marijuana. Cocaine use rose steadily but gradually, and leveled off in 1998, but is still less than half of what it was in the peak year of 1986. Although crack use never reached the epidemic proportions that had been predicted, it is moving from the inner cities, where its effects have been devastating, into affluent suburbs, and among some eighth-graders use has gone up slightly. Nevertheless, relatively few teenagers use either powdered cocaine or crack. In general, drug use seems to be leveling off or even declining slightly, and eighth-graders who increasingly disapprove of drug users provide hope that the new epidemic that began in 1991 will gradually subside. The scattered declines in use and changes in attitude are modest, but hopeful.

Along with some encouraging trends, there is bad news. The percentage of high school students who smoke has gone up a third since 1991. The rate of experimentation with a wide variety of drugs is still several times higher than it was just a few years ago. Heroin use, although quite low, rose significantly among eighth-, tenth-, and twelfth-graders during the mid-1990s. This rise may be a reflection of the fact that the drug is now so pure it does not have to be injected but can be smoked, swallowed or snorted for a quick high, and many youngsters believe mistakenly that only injection leads to addiction. Use has dropped slightly for twelfth-graders, but is still rising for younger children. Obviously, this is no time for complacency. The statistics, while generally moving in the right direction, indicate only a slight drop or leveling-off from extreme levels—like a fever that dips from 104 degrees to 102 degrees and has a long way to go before it signals the return of health. The United States continues to have the highest level of illicit drug use in the world, and the true figures are undoubtedly higher, since school dropouts (who are most likely to be drug users) are not counted in standard surveys. So when your teenager says that "everybody's doing it," he or she is not far wrong.

Yet there is also another reality. More than half of all high school seniors have not even tried marijuana. Even alcohol use is not inevitable. One young woman who grew up in Maryland says, "I didn't drink at all in high school. In my school the 'good kids' didn't drink. I didn't find out until I was in college that there were kids who got good grades and also drank."

But in other schools and among other groups of friends your child's perceptions that substance abuse is everywhere may be accurate. As Dr. John Q. Lantry, former principal of Round Hill Elementary School in Washingtonville, New York, put it, "If they don't want to follow their friends, they're bucking one hell of a trend."

Favorite drugs differ from place to place and even from school to school. In 1995 in Indiana, LSD use increased abruptly. In the South and Southwest, Rohypnol, known as "roofies" and imported from Mexico, gained in popularity.

This sedative, legal in many countries but banned in the United States, is ten times more powerful than Valium. Often used in combination with alcohol, it can be slipped into the drinks of unsuspecting young women, who pass out and are then "date-raped." After the event, they remember nothing. On the West Coast, methamphetamine—often called "L.A. ice"—is a fast-growing favorite. Called "the poor man's cocaine" and ferociously addictive, it is starting to spread across the country as crack cocaine did in the eighties, threatening to become the most destructive drug of the nineties.

Cocaine is a special case and presents special dangers. It used to be an elite drug, used in small quantities by small numbers of people who had the money to buy it. Now it is cheaper, widely available, widely used, and finally recognized by those with experience in the field as dangerously addictive and more lethal than heroin. Recognition of its dangers by inner-city youth themselves may help explain the sharp decrease in the use of crack cocaine in the late eighties. In the nineties, it started a slow drift upward.

Heroin, which used to be seen as the drug used only by inner-city "junkies" who had essentially dropped out of life, is making a frightening appearance among suburban youth. In Plano, Texas, an upscale suburb twenty miles north of Dallas, nine youngsters died of heroin overdoses within two years. The drug's cheapness, and the fact that it no longer has to be injected, are credited by drug experts with almost doubling the number of high school students nationally who used it between 1992 and 1997. The percentage is small, and in 1998 there was a small drop in these figures, but any use is disturbing.

LOOKING AHEAD TO WORK OR COLLEGE

If your child has had experience with alcohol and drugs in high school, or even if he or she has escaped the worst of the current epidemic, you may be worried about what will happen when your youngster enters the wider world. For many young people, the transition is a rough one. They often find themselves away from home, without the social props of longtime friends and family, living with people whose standards and activities may be quite different from those they knew earlier. The sense of freedom can be exhilarating, and the urge to experiment is strong and natural. Most communities, like college campuses, provide easy access to the whole array of today's drugs and alcohol, and the past offers few guidelines. Military service is one away-from-home option that is less likely to propel a young adult into drug use. The services have taken a strong stand against any drug use, with expulsion the penalty for disobeying this regulation.

What was true for earlier graduating classes is no longer true for today's. Drug use has changed. Hallucinogens are again becoming fashionable, and marijuana is often smoked as casually as tobacco used to be. As one Oregon teenager put it, "It's easy to do, easy to grow, easy to get, and easy to sell. . . . When you go to a concert or go dancing, the thing to do is smoke dope." In what Dr. Lloyd D. Johnston of the University of Michigan's Monitoring the Future study calls "generational forgetting," students today have not been exposed to the horrors of bad trips and wasted lives that kept some youngsters away from the dangerous drugs used by their older brothers and sisters, and acceptance of drug use has exploded. But for some drugs, this acceptance now seems to be dropping slightly. In 1998 there was a small increase in the perception of the dangers of using ampheta-mines and marijuana. On the other hand, eighth-graders were less likely than they had been to see LSD use as risky. But nothing can compare to alcohol.

As a Connecticut student wrote in the irreverent *The Insider's Guide to the Colleges* (compiled and edited by the staff of the *Yale Daily News*), for many, drinking is the weekend activity of choice. Weekends run from Thursday through Saturday, with Sunday as the time to recoup before going back to the academic pressures of the abbreviated school week. Some partying students try not to schedule Friday classes. Others stumble into class hungover or still drunk. Forty percent of college students report they have binged in the past two weeks.

Students on many campuses divide into groups—some are devotees of "raves," the all-night dance parties where drug use is cultivated; others are "conservative," more likely to belong to sororities and fraternities, and drink a lot. In one month, five Virginia college students were killed in alcohol-related accidents. One, a young woman who was a senior honors student, was found lying at the bottom of a flight of stairs and later died in a hospital. Her blood-alcohol level was more than three times the legal driving limit.

The reality that you don't have to be alcoholic to have alcohol kill you has frightened some students into abstinence. The general climate of "temperance" has also played a part in lowering college drinking. In 1980, 9.5 percent of college students said they did not drink at all; in 1996, the figure was 17 percent. Counselors report that students today are likely to be either abstainers or binge drinkers; the moderate middle seems to have disappeared. But students say that setting twenty-one as the drinking age hasn't had much effect. They learned in high school about false IDs, and school rules, such as requiring that someone over twenty-one be responsible at on-campus parties, are not hard to circumvent. At the University of Virginia in 1997, three to ten students landed in the emergency room with alcohol poisoning each weekend; 70 percent of them were too young to drink legally.

You can help your child understand when choosing a college that at a career-oriented school with a highly organized social life there will be pressure to drink and that drug taking may be more common at nontraditional colleges. (*The Insider's Guide to the Colleges* provides specific information about what is to be found at each school.) The question he or she will have to consider is which would be more comfortable. Will your child's sharing a dormitory room with a drug user be disturbing, even if your child does not fall into that pattern?

One young woman found herself at a college where hallucinogens were popular. First she encountered psychedelic mushrooms, and then LSD. Her college roommate, who seemed "one of the most together people I ever knew—outgoing, popular, everyone liked her," took LSD. One night, under the influence of the drug, she tried to clean the communal bathroom with her toothbrush, and screamed and talked until dawn. After three days during which she talked to herself and felt she had a mission to help the people of the world, she was persuaded to see a counselor. Finally, she was hospitalized in a local psychiatric unit, where she remained for months. "It destroyed the second semester of my freshman year," her roommate says. "I had to transfer to another school."

WHAT'S HAPPENING IN YOUR COMMUNITY?

Just as colleges are different, each community has its unique characteristics. National publications may alert you to the dangers of designer drugs or homemade PCP (angel dust), and those substances may or may not be of major concern in your area. Usually a drug fad will start on one coast or the other, and then filter to the middle of the country. But there may be local favorites, based on availability, price, and how vigorously they are being pushed.

Here's how you can tell what's really going on:

1. Listen to your kids when they talk to you and when they talk to their friends. You don't have to be a spy—just stay alert. If after every weekend you hear jokes about who was "smashed," you know there's a lot of drinking going on. One boy just happened to pick up the extension when his fifteen-year-old older brother was on the phone planning an afternoon at a friend's house. "Bring some booze—we're all out" is what he heard. The older boy said he couldn't get anything from the liquor cabinet because too many people were around. The younger boy told his mother. (Whether he should have or not is a decision each family has to make.) She picked her older son up earlier than planned, and talked with him calmly about what his friends were doing. She'd had no idea before this that they spent Saturday afternoons drinking.

2. Read your local, school, and college papers if they're available. From news stories, letters to the editor, even cartoons, you will find out what's happening. Be sensitive to what is not completely spelled out. After the son of the 1984 vice-presidential nominee Geraldine Ferraro

was arrested for possession of and intent to sell cocaine, reporters learned that his fellow college students had been suspicious for a long time. The April Fool edition of the college newspaper had carried a mock advertisement with a picture of the young man and the line "My mom may drink Pepsi [Ferraro had done a Pepsi commercial] but I like Coke." Below this was "Changing in line with the times." College officials seemed neither to notice nor to understand the reference. It was easier and more comfortable to avoid facing the existence of drug use on campus, despite public pronouncements about official disapproval.

3. Talk to other parents. Like college officials, parents may want both to know and not to know, and trying to get information may be difficult. But it's worth the effort. An example of how ostrich-like parents can be was revealed when the Partnership for a Drug-Free America polled children, teenagers, and their parents across the country. Only 21 percent of the parents thought their teenagers had experimented with marijuana, yet 44 percent of the teenagers said they had done so. Even though many of these parents had lived through the drug-filled sixties, they were as naive as parents of the past. They were unaware that marijuana use had increased, that children and teenagers found it easier to get, and that among young people awareness of the risks of the drug decreased. (That decrease has now leveled off and, at least among eighth-graders, is even declining slightly, a hopeful sign for the future.)

4. Go to school and community meetings on the subject of alcohol and drugs, even if your kid says, "Please don't go. You'll embarrass me."

5. Notice what your local stores are selling. Head shops stocked with drug paraphernalia and cigarette-rolling papers in the stationery store are a sure sign of local use. So are magazines about drugs.

6. Check the Internet for what information—and propaganda—there is about drinking and drug-making and -taking. One website to look into is that for *High Times*, the monthly magazine about drugs. In addition, more than thirty-five alcohol brands have their own websites. As for tobacco, more than fifty websites praise the wonders of smoking for women. Chances are your kids have found one or more of these sites.

7. Keep your eyes open at parties in the neighborhood or at your house. If you see volunteers overeager to clean up afterward (to remove signs of smoking or drinking from the back lawn or the family room), be suspicious. Awareness is the first step toward doing something about your child's exposure to alcohol and other drugs.

2

Why My Kid?

You say, "My kid can't be chemically dependent." You think, "I've done all the right things." We made Play-Doh toys together. I kept score at Rich's baseball games. I was doing all these things, the right things, so that means it couldn't be happening to me.

—A MINNESOTA MOTHER

If parents could protect their children against the devastating effects of drugs, nicotine, and alcohol as easily as they can protect them against measles and polio, they would rush to do whatever was necessary. But life is not that simple. There's no vaccine that guarantees against substance abuse, or any simple test to show who will succumb.

Although studies indicate no addictive personality in the clinical sense, some youngsters are clearly more likely than others to be attracted to and hooked on drugs, nicotine, and alcohol. Experts agree that both internal, personal factors and external, environmental ones are involved in tipping the scale in one direction or another.

The risks are greater if a cluster of these conditions exists:

Family History

- A close relative with a history of alcoholism
- A parent who uses drugs
- A family in turmoil; for instance, one dealing with serious dissension, death, divorce

Personal History

- Behavioral problems before adolescence
- Early school failure
- Early sexual activity (particularly for girls)
- Hyperactivity
- Learning difficulties
- Dependence on others for leadership and direction

Beliefs

- "It can't happen to me. I can control drug or alcohol use."
- "What I use or don't use is my choice, and it is my right to make that choice."
- "What I do with my body is my business."
- "Cocaine (or marijuana or another drug) is not addictive or harmful, despite information to the contrary."
- "My friends think it is okay, and so do I."

Personality Factors

- Poor impulse control
- Rebelliousness
- Low self-image
- Inability to delay gratification
- Impatience with the slow process of growing up

Of course, some kids whose parents have divorced or who can hardly wait until they are old enough to drive or to date don't run into trouble, while others now coming into treatment don't fit into the usual risk categories. If a child does use drugs, it is not necessarily a personal failure on the part of the parent. Some kids are more susceptible to use and abuse because of a fragile nervous system or genetic vulnerability. Others experiment and never have any problems. Parents can take neither all the credit nor all the blame.

FAMILY HISTORY

One family thread in the background of many young alcohol and drug abusers is alcoholism. The children of alcoholics are three to four times more likely to become alcoholic than other children. Mounting evidence, through studies of identical twins and the brain waves of young children, suggests that a genetic predisposition may be involved.

If you have a history of alcoholism in your family, you should reveal the "terrible secret" to your children. They must know that they have a greater chance of getting hooked. Their decision to use drugs and alcohol will then be a conscious one. Alcoholism is as much a part of their health history as knowing that a grandfather had diabetes or a grandmother had breast cancer.

DRUG-USING PARENTS

Drug use is also often a problem among youngsters whose parents grew up in the sixties and still use drugs themselves. Studies show that children of such parents are much more likely than other children to abuse chemical substances. Among youngsters calling the 800-COCAINE Hotline because they were concerned about their own involvement, 40 percent had parents who used marijuana or other illicit drugs.

Many parents who have used drugs—or are still using them—now find themselves worried about their own children's attraction to substances they themselves helped popularize, yet they are often ambivalent about the dangers of some drugs based on their own experiences. This very ambivalence can push a child into use. Without a firm parental stand, the likelihood of drug involvement increases.

If you find yourself confused about what to say to your children, remember that times have changed. Mary Ann, who went through the sixties in San Francisco, the capital of the drug world, says, "Our pot use was more a political statement than it is now. We only found out later, 'Gee, this stuff is addictive.' Heavy use for us was three times a week, not three joints a day. And there's a real difference in the strength of the marijuana we smoked."

She is now concerned about her fourteen-year-old daughter, who saw her parents smoking pot at parties when she was younger. "I tell her I don't want her to do it, in the same way I don't want her to smoke cigarettes or eat sugar," she says. But she acknowledges that her daughter will probably experiment and has suggested that if she wants to try it once, "she should let me know. I can get pure stuff and avoid the dangers of marijuana contaminated by things like PCP."

Although it sounds sensible, Mary Ann's attitude is hazardous. The double message—"I don't want you to use it, but it's safer if it's good stuff"—can sound like parental approval. And, in a sense, it is. A father with a similar viewpoint who was in the motion-picture business and said he'd had "cocaine around him forever" decided to teach his daughter to use drugs "responsibly" when she was in her midteens. They smoked pot together and used a little cocaine. It was part of father-daughter communication, he thought. Now he has stopped using drugs—but she has become addicted.

If, like almost half of all baby-boomer parents, you experimented with or used marijuana or other illicit substances regularly when you were younger, you may be dreading the time when your child will want to know about your drug history. On the other hand, you may be depending on the typical adolescent indifference to a parents' past to keep the subject from ever coming up. Parents like you are more likely than other parents to expect their children to be users and report feeling helpless to prevent this use, perhaps echoing their experience with their own parents. Unfortunately, evading responsibility for your children's drug use—"Nothing I do or say can have any effect"—makes it more likely that they will succumb to temptation.

You may feel, along with the mother of two girls, eight

and fourteen, that you won't say you used unless your children ask directly—a kind of "if they don't ask, don't tell" attitude. Other parents interviewed for a nationwide study overwhelmingly said they would tell their children. There are no clear-cut rules. Certainly, your child must know how you feel about drug use, but whether—and how—you tell your own story depends on your relationship with your child, the child's age, and the way the question comes up. More than seventy million adults—including the president, the vice president, and the former Speaker of the House of Representatives—have used marijuana at some time in their lives. As Patrick McGowan, sheriff of Hennepin County, Minnesota, points out, "As a society we have removed the stigma from marijuana use and now we face a very tough job of convincing our young people that we are serious when we tell them this is unacceptable."

Some parents believe that discussing their own use makes their children feel that the parents understand what the teenagers are going through. Others are reluctant to reveal themselves because they know their children are just waiting to catch them at one more thing that justifies their critical view of adults. The parent who admits to use, but tells his children to stay away from it, runs the risk of being seen as hypocritical by teens who are acutely attuned to adult imperfections. Then again, if you were one of those who didn't use (and remember you were in the majority, although the assumption is that everyone used in the sixties and seventies), your warnings may be dismissed because "you don't know anything about it."

It sounds like a no-win situation. But there are things you can say that will make clear why you don't want your child to use, and will not shut the door on further discussion. One mother said when asked, "I used it. It was stupid. It interfered with my schoolwork and my friendships, so I just stopped doing it." You can tell your child you hope he or she will be smarter than you were, and that whatever happens you can still talk about it. Remember that behind your child's stated question is the unspoken one: "What should I do?" rather than what did you do.

If you did use, there's no need to go into great detail about your experiences with drugs, any more than your child needs to hear details of your financial status or sexual history. Just as with any other guidance you provide, you have to tailor your approach to the age of the child, and wait for a "teachable moment." Perhaps your twelve-year-old will come home from school and report that the teacher said it was pretty common for people of your generation to use drugs. You might say, "Yes, many did. But they were a lot older than you are—in their late teens and twenties. Things are very different today. The drugs are stronger, and the kids are younger." If you are asked directly if you used, you have to be quite clear in your own mind about whether you will tell the truth or sidestep the subject. Think about it long before you are confronted with the situation, and rehearse in your mind how you will handle it. How much do you want them to know? What will best prepare them to avoid the dangers of drug use? How honest do you expect them to be about their own use?

Some parents try to hide their drug use from their children, expecting this to protect them from being tempted. A mother who returned from a vacation to find an empty liquor closet and burns on the couch said, "I don't get it. We never smoked pot in front of them. And we told them again and again not to do it." As a parent you have to remember that kids know what's going on behind closed doors, whether it is arguing or drug-using. And they imitate what you do, not what you say. But if you are currently using marijuana or other illicit drugs and are convinced your child doesn't know, the experts agree you should not say anything unless you are confronted directly. When that happens, you cannot continue to sidestep but must answer the question. You should then get help for both of you in dealing with the situation.

What can you do if the parents of your child's best friend smoke marijuana or use other drugs at home? You can, of course, forbid your child to go there. But this may backfire in increasing rebellion and furtive visits. On the other hand, your youngster may be relieved to be removed from difficult circumstances by being told, "That house is absolutely off limits." At the very least, you need to let your child know that you don't like what goes on in that household, and discourage visits.

Even if they don't use drugs or drink too much, parents give unwitting messages by their actions. They say "Don't drink" and then celebrate every important occasion by getting "pleasantly high." Even young children pay attention and show it in subtle ways. When two six-year-old girls tired of playing with stuffed animals, one said, "Now what should we do?" and her friend suggested, "Let's play drunk."

Some parents tell their children to stay away from drugs as if they were the plague, then reach for a pill at every twinge of discomfort. They unconsciously encourage flouting the law by casually not paying income taxes ("Everyone cheats on taxes"), running a red light ("Let's see if we can get away with this one"), or stealing ("Don't get caught"), and then are dismayed when youngsters circumvent the legal drinking age. Studies show that examples set by parents and older brothers and sisters often influence teenagers to use or not to use drugs. This influence can be unexpected and widespread. One study concluded, "When mothers are cigarette smokers . . . teenage children are more likely to use a variety of drugs."

Kids are worried by parental behavior. One girl in an affluent suburb turned in a panic to her school counselor when she discovered syringes in her mother's jewelry box, and suspected for the first time that her mother was using drugs. Other youngsters have told police officers who conduct DARE (Drug Abuse Resistance Education) drug prevention programs in schools that they are afraid of being hurt by their drinking or drug-using parents. Reports of parents smoking marijuana in front of their children are also widespread. The change in attitude among adults in certain social circles that now accept such use as "no big deal" is reflected in a sharp change in the attitude of children as well. A 1996 nationwide survey by the Partnership for a Drug-Free America found a marked increase in the number of youngsters nine to twelve years old who were less likely than their counterparts two year earlier to think it risky to use drugs, and more likely to experiment. Paradoxically, some parents may think it is all right for adults to use marijuana but wrong for children; children may think it is not terribly risky for young people to smoke pot, but a real problem if parents do.

Since a parent's use of alcohol, tobacco, marijuana, and prescription and nonprescription drugs can affect children's behavior, an honest look at your own attitudes and actions can help your kids. Here are some questions, distributed by the University of Wisconsin, to guide you toward seeing yourself more clearly. A positive answer doesn't mean you have to see yourself as an unfit parent, but you should be aware that what you do influences your child.

- When you have a headache, do you immediately take a pill to get rid of the pain?
- When you are nervous or upset, is your immediate response to "take something" to get rid of the feeling?
- Do your children ever hear you arguing about one or the other having had too much to drink?
- Have you ever warned your children about smoking while you were smoking? How about drinking?
- Do you smoke marijuana?
- Do you handle alcohol or any other drugs in a way that you would not want your children to?

You should also be aware that involving your child in your own use of alcohol and other drugs can increase his chances of becoming a user. You shouldn't ask a child to light your cigarette or get a beer from the refrigerator or pass drinks around at a party.

THE CHILD'S PERSONAL HISTORY

In addition to family considerations, some children have personal histories that should alert you to potential drug use. Connie knew her son wasn't like other children by the time he was in third grade. "He flunked lunch," she says.

"He was belligerent. He kicked other kids." He went to a center for psychological evaluation, and "there's one thing in the report I'll always remember," she says. "There was a note that said 'considering these characteristics, this person may have trouble with alcohol.' "

The report was right. Timmy went to eight different schools, including one for "underachievers," in the hope that his academic performance would improve and he would settle down. "But," says his mother sadly, "it was like being on an island and hearing a hurricane coming. You batten down and do everything and nothing helps." He started taking liquor out of the liquor cabinet, using other drugs, and stealing the car at night to subvert his parents' attempts to monitor him. Now, at age seventeen, he is in inpatient treatment, and his father has had to face the fact that there is alcoholism in his family and that he, too, sometimes drinks too much.

Kids who have learning difficulties sometimes turn to drugs, as Timmy did. Help with this aspect of their lives can make them feel more adequate and less likely to succumb to temptation, but, obviously, there is no guarantee. Timmy's mother may have been right when she felt that she was at the mercy of forces she could not control. Dr. Mitchell Rosenthal, president of Phoenix House, says, "A significant number of kids in treatment have learning problems. They feel stupid and see themselves as unable to handle things in school. Drug use certainly worsens the problem." It is sometimes hard to know whether the learning disability or the drug use came first.

A danger exists, however, if a catch-all diagnosis of learning disabilities is used by experts and parents to avoid the real problem—drug use, which dulls the brain and interferes with concentration. In young children, though, who are nowhere near the age of drug use, help with schoolwork can sometimes make a big difference. Very early school problems should not be ignored. The director of a substance abuse program in a large school system says he can identify in second grade three-quarters of the children who are at high risk of using alcohol and drugs when they reach middle school.

PERSONALITY FACTORS

Of course, it is a lot easier to bring up a child who is calm, respectful, and obedient than one who is rebellious and demanding. Although impulsivity, an "I want what I want when I want it" attitude, doesn't cause drug abuse, it may make it more likely that drugs, which provide instant gratification, will seem attractive. In other cases, when the personalities of parents and children conflict, tensions rise and can set the stage for drug use. The exuberant, athletic father and the shy, book-loving son may find themselves at odds because of inborn temperamental differences. Then, too, the need to develop a separate identity, to go from being a dependent child to being an independent adult, puts children into a push-pull relationship with parents that often feels like an angry tug-of-war. But what seems like rebellion may really be a child's way of saying, "I don't know who I am, but this I do know—I am not you. I'm different." The child rejects parental attitudes and expectations on the road to developing his own ideas and personality.

WHO ABUSES DRUGS?

Peer pressure during the teenage years is at the top of the list of factors pushing youngsters into experimenting with drugs, according to Dr. D. Vincent Biase, former director of research and development at Daytop Village, a leading drug treatment center. But it shouldn't be blamed for drug abuse, which is usually the result of internal unhappiness in addition to the drive toward social acceptability.

Kids see drug and alcohol use as a part of being grown-up. In addition, drug use and drinking are considered something to do like cruising around in a car or hanging out on a street corner. Kids also use because they want to do what their friends do, are bored, like the way it feels, or are just curious. Some middle-class youngsters feel resentful that they've been sheltered and protected almost to psychic death. One of them says, "I know there's a lot more to life than I've experienced. The sixties music is wonderful and they talk a lot about drugs, so you begin to wonder, 'What am I missing?' "

But youngsters who abuse drugs add other reasons to this list. Billy says he got deeply involved "because I thought my world was shit and I didn't think much of myself, either." He got drunk for the first time in sixth grade and by ninth grade was smoking marijuana every day and using "everything I could get my hands on." In tenth grade he tried LSD and liked it. When his mother asked if he was "on something" he countered with the standard "How could you accuse me?" His father thought it was just a stage. Billy dropped out of his first treatment program, and swore he would never smoke again, but is finally back in treatment after his parents threatened to kick him out.

Like Billy, youngsters who use drugs as medication to counteract sadness or blot out intolerable home situations are more likely than others to become dependent on chemicals to get through the day. One of them says, "I have so many bad feelings that I get high because I want to feel better." The dangerous thing about drugs is that they work—at least for a while. Dr. Rodney Skager, professor emeritus at UCLA, says they not only help kids feel better, smoothing some of the normal jagged feelings of adolescence, but they also help them feel different—more capable, more likable, more complete. During the honeymoon period, drugs seem to do all the good things they are supposed to do, and none of the bad. These first tries are usually guided by more practiced friends. They help the novices enjoy the experience, and shield them so they don't see any frightening effects. Therefore, they don't believe their parents' warnings.

Youngsters seem to select a particular drug because it does what they need it to do. If they are frequent users, they often have a favorite and resist switching. Some adolescents also avoid certain drugs. On a larger scale, one counselor points out that "drugs fit the times. Marijuana was a sixties drug because it makes you mellow. Coke was the eighties drug because it speeds you up." In the nineties it is not one drug that characterizes the decade but the effect any number of drugs can produce: oblivion. Kids now sniff inhalants until they pass out, drink to become unconscious, and smoke enough marijuana to blot out a world that seems too hard to deal with. For Dr. Herbert Kleber, medical director of the National Center on Addiction and Substance Abuse, the marked increase in marijuana use and the resurgence of heroin are the most troubling trends of the nineties.

Boys and girls smoke cigarettes at about the same alarming rate. By the end of high school almost a fourth are smoking daily. But they seem to differ in their choice of drugs other than tobacco. Boys are more likely than girls to fasten on large quantities of alcohol, particularly beer, as their drug of choice. It has a macho image, and reduces inhibitions so that its users can feel powerful around girls, take wild chances, and seem fearless. Girls are more likely to use amphetamines and often start with them for weight control. They measure their worth by their beauty, and equate beauty with slimness.

Linda, blond and blue-eyed, called herself "queen of the world," but at seventeen she died of an overdose of Dexedrine and heroin. She had become anorexic and bulimic at fourteen, starving herself into "beauty" after her parents divorced. At fifteen she discovered that amphetamines could help push her weight even lower. Her drug habits became so expensive that she turned to prostitution. One night her boyfriend found her unconscious in his apartment, but he was too late to revive her.

WHY SOME KIDS DON'T USE

Parents are often puzzled because one or two children in a family get involved and the others stay out of the drug picture. They say, "My parenting worked with the others— why not with this one?" But each child has a different personality and experiences a different family. Parents react uniquely to each son and daughter, sometimes seeing in one the characteristics that are "just like Uncle Ed, who was always in trouble," while in another, they see the best qualities of themselves or their spouses. The children also fit differently into the family, some more comfortably than others. A lot depends on luck and how strong a sense of self the child has developed.

In the search for understanding why some youngsters avoid the dangers that ensnare others, investigators have come up with one intriguing finding: Children who do well in spite of difficulties often have a close tie to an adult other than a parent—an aunt, uncle, grandparent, teacher, or family friend. Finding another person in whom to confide may be a boon for a particular child, although a parent may feel hurt and rejected. In the long run, the relationship with this surrogate figure may make the difference between a kid who falls by the wayside and one who resists temptation.

About 30 percent of California's eleventh-graders were "highly resistant to drug and alcohol use," according to a study made a decade ago for the attorney general of the state. These hard-core nonusers tended to share the attitude that using "is not me." They said no not because their parents were against it or because of the dangers but because their pictures of themselves didn't include the use of alcohol and other drugs, and they were able to stick with this inner vision.

More recently, an innovative approach to combating the ravages of alcohol abuse among children on Indian reservations has involved harnessing the same powerful internal forces. Tribal officials have launched an educational campaign reminding young people that alcohol was introduced by white men and is not part of their traditional practices. Drunkenness is not inevitable on the road to manhood. The message is beginning to get through, with chapters of Students Against Driving Drunk growing rapidly. Another culturally based attack has been aimed at smoking among African Americans. To counteract tobacco companies' campaigns directed at black youth, a New York City group ran ads with a pointed, personal message: "They used to make us pick it. Now they want us to smoke it." Tobacco use was not only "not me" but "not us." Cigarette smoking by African American teens plummeted for twenty years, then rose a precipitous 80 percent between 1991 and 1998. Experts explained the rise by citing the glamorization of cigarettes and cigars, the stable price of tobacco products, and concerted advertising directed at black teens. Nevertheless, rates stayed well below those of white teens. While 40 percent of white female teens smoke, only 17 percent of black female students do.

Why one child has an internal compass and another doesn't is still a puzzle. But there are some clues. Children who feel "connected" to their parents and to their schools, one 1995 federal study of students in grades seven through twelve showed, were less likely to use alcohol, tobacco, and marijuana. And the presence of a parent at key times during the day—in the morning, after school, at dinner, at bedtime—also reduced the chance that a child would use drugs. (Since 1960, children have lost an average of ten to twelve hours of parental time each week.) But a parent's "being there" emotionally by showing warmth, love, and caring was by far the most important factor, even more important than the amount of time spent at home or whether the child came from a one- or two-parent family. As one of the researchers put it, "Parents are just as important to adolescents as they are to smaller children." But Joy Dryfoos, author of *Safe Passage: Making It Through Adolescence in a Risky Society*, cautions that "Parents can't just decide one day to turn on the warmth and caring and then feel they've done the job. Their involvement has to begin early and continue through the child's life. If they can't do it they had better make sure that somebody else can, whether it is another adult or an institution such as the school."

In general, research shows that children who do not abuse drugs share certain characteristics. They are likely to be resilient and easygoing; have strong ties to their parents or other adults; understand that drug and alcohol use is unacceptable according to family rules; and know that their parents expect them to do well academically. Some children who avoid drugs and alcohol come from family backgrounds in which religion is very important. They say they do not use because "it is morally wrong." A child who has deeply held religious beliefs is less likely than other youngsters to drink, smoke, or use illicit drugs.

Whatever parents do, neither drug use nor avoidance of it is inevitable. Even the children of former Flower Children do not necessarily become users or abusers. Dr. David Smith of San Francisco's Haight-Ashbury Free Clinic has watched this country's love affair with drugs for almost thirty years, and he says of such children, "Some are punk rockers strung out on speed, but others are a lot more conservative than their parents. They're health freaks and don't use anything. They think something that's harmful is red meat."

DENIAL

No parent likes to acknowledge that his child might be a drug user. It seems to be an admission of failure as a parent and is a frightening recognition that something must be done. To avoid this painful possibility, parents cover up, avoid seeing what is obvious to others, or deny the extent of the problem. "Secrecy is the biggest enemy," one father of a drug-abusing boy told *Washingtonian Magazine.* "In trying to keep anybody from knowing what was going on in our family, we reached the point where we didn't know ourselves."

A policeman in Deerfield, Illinois, has his own method for waking parents up to the truth. "If I find a kid drinking in a car," he says, "parents don't believe me unless I call them and tell them to come down and pick the kid up. There's a lot of denial, and I've really become tough."

Parents also can inadvertently prolong the drug use. One mother says, "We did everything. We made excuses for him when he cut school. We got him a tutor when he was failing. We arranged for saxophone lessons because that was something he liked and we thought he would be less angry. Only after we recognized that drugs were the problem did we learn he and his music teacher had been doing cocaine together."

Counselors see covering up, making excuses, and sidestepping reality as enabling. Parents often play this role out of love. Unfortunately, what they actually accomplish is to derail the process leading toward recovery. If they have a family history of alcoholism, they have often seen enabling at work, and as adults are more likely than others to deny there is a problem. They may have heard their mother call their father's employer and say, "He has a virus," when he was really hungover.

One grown daughter of an alcoholic father really didn't

want to know what was going on with her own teenage daughter. Even when she found that liquor was missing, she never mentioned it. She just took the nearly empty bottle of Amaretto and put it on top of the refrigerator—"then she knew that I knew." The conspiracy of silence in this house was particularly strong because the alcoholic grandfather ("he's not that bad") was living in the downstairs apartment of his daughter's house.

A father whose own father "had a drinking problem" didn't recognize what was going on with his drug- and alcohol-abusing son for ten years. "Then I didn't just wake up one day and realize it. It happened slowly, inch by inch. I knew something was wrong. His grades dropped, we were fighting at home, but I didn't see what it was," he says. According to Joan Duncan, formerly director of family services at the Monmouth Chemical Dependency Treatment Center in Long Branch, New Jersey, "Parents usually accept the possibility of drug and alcohol abuse only as a last resort."

If you yourself are the child of a drug abuser or alcoholic you undoubtedly know from personal experience how hard it is to grow up in a chaotic household. The child and grandchild of alcoholic men says, "The thing I always question is, how do you be a good mother? How much of what I do is because I feel guilty? I'm constantly looking to see who is a good parent—where can I find a model?"

Uncertain parents such as this mother have to be particularly careful that they don't overreact to their child's experimental use of alcohol or drugs, or feel helpless if they can't "fix" the child as they desperately wished to fix the alcoholic parent.

WHERE DID I GO WRONG?

Parents see their children as report cards on their parenting ability. When a child runs into trouble, parents torment themselves: "What did I do wrong? Was there some point when I could have done this instead of that and kept the whole mess from happening?" The truth is, children develop in a particular way because of a multitude of factors, including inborn temperament, the circumstances in which they grew up, the social climate and times in which they live, their families, and more.

Mothers most often take the blame, the unbearable pain, and the guilt on themselves, while fathers and experts have often supported and intensified the mother's own self-criticism. Says one psychotherapist, "There's been a conspiracy in psychiatry, 'Hang the mother.' It's our version of witchhunting."

In recent years, a more realistic attitude has been taking hold, with the realization that fathers, too, have an enormous impact. Fathers are now routinely invited into delivery rooms to hold their newborn babies and bond with them. They are also being criticized for focusing their energies on their careers and neglecting their children's need for emotional as well as financial support.

Despite heroic efforts, all any parent can be is what a Long Island social worker, echoing the English psychoanalyst D. W. Winnicott, calls "good enough." He says, "We all make mistakes." A father put it more bluntly: "I screwed up as a parent and I did my best." No matter how hard we try, at times, nothing seems to help. When our children are infants, we do our best to protect them from falling downstairs or touching a hot stove. But as they get older, our protective shield becomes less effective. Our children hook up with the wrong friends, are hurt by life's ordinary blows, and even run away or try suicide. We feel helpless and sad when they meet the world on their own and fail—by our standards and by theirs, too. Religion can be a steadying force. If you are a person with strong religious convictions, you certainly should turn to your clergyman for guidance or rededication to your faith. Belief in a "higher power" is very much a part of recovery for some people. Prayer alone cannot be counted on, but it can certainly hold out hope and comfort.

Instead of assigning blame, a parent has to have the courage to say to a child, "Something did go wrong—mistakes were made and you were hurt. But we didn't intend this to happen, and we are all victims of forces that we're unaware of and can't control." It isn't helpful to beat yourself with what a mother called the "if only" whip—"If only I had stayed home more." "If only my husband hadn't lost his temper so often." "If only we had gotten her into treatment the minute we suspected."

Yet it is only natural that you should feel disappointed in your child and in yourself when things don't go smoothly. The mother of a twenty-two-year-old man says, "I couldn't understand what had happened to me and to my child, who was so full of promise. He was such a great little kid." Youngsters who start using drugs are not all failures; some are honor students and star athletes, so the loss of what might have been is stunning. The discrepancy is often beyond understanding.

When a child becomes deeply involved with alcohol and drugs, parents go through a period of mourning for what was and what could have been. "I look at old pictures, old letters, and cry for the child he was," said the mother of a heroin addict. "The loss of the dream is a horror."

Sometimes the dream is only deferred until recovery moves life back into its earlier pattern. But sometimes the child will never fulfill that early promise. "Nothing can be more hurtful than to see a child going through this," says one mother. "Something in me thought it was just a stage and he would be a normal kid again. The irrational part of me still thinks he will come out of it. But then I realize he will always be damaged."

"I felt so horrible," the father of a boy who had used "the whole smorgasbord of drugs" recalls, "that I wished he would die somehow and we could bury him and avoid the shame and struggle of having to deal with it. I guess that's what you call guilt."

UNDERSTANDING THE GUILT

You may feel guilty, too. One thing to realize is that it is a sign of maturity to be able to carry some guilt. We all do. It cannot be wiped out, but you can accept remorse as part of the human condition. Without it we would be living in a chaotic world in which no one cared.

Sometimes guilt can be a useful emotion. "Guilt is like a fever," says Emily Shachter, a Rockland County, New York, psychotherapist who specializes in the treatment of children. "It can warn you that something is wrong and has to be taken care of."

Guilt can also be crippling. Instead of letting children feel the consequences of their actions, guilty parents say,

"It's really my fault. I'll pay for the broken window," and the destructive behavior continues.

Understanding and transmuting guilt can be liberating. The psychoanalyst Alice Miller writes, "The realization that even with the best will in the world we are not omnipotent, that we are subject to compulsions, and that we cannot love our child in the way we would like may lead to sorrow but should not awaken guilt feelings, because the latter imply a power and freedom we do not have."

In a way, guilt is catching, since it also burdens the children with uncomfortable feelings. Dr. Miller suggests that mourning is a more appropriate reaction. "It is an expression of pain that things happened as they did and that there is no way to change the past. We can share this pain with our children without having to feel ashamed."

The pain is sometimes so overwhelming that it feels physical. It may settle in your stomach or your chest. It may feel as if it will never go away. But time tempers even this kind of anguish, and although everyone's timetable is different, the one certainty in life is that things will change.

3

Warning Signs

Most of us adults wouldn't recognize a stoned kid if he was carrying a candy bar in one hand and a bottle of eye drops in another.

—DR. JOHN E. MEEKS, PSYCHIATRIC INSTITUTE OF
MONTGOMERY COUNTY, MARYLAND

Some parents go through their children's adolescence in a state of hysteria, sure that the worst is about to happen. Others refuse to face obvious problems. Even normal adolescence can be turbulent. Dr. Everett Dulit, director of adolescent psychiatry at Albert Einstein Medical Center in New York, points out, "Being outrageous is one of the pleasures of adolescence." These days, with so much that used to be shocking now commonplace, it takes a lot more than four-letter words to shake up the adult world. Drug use is one of the ways youngsters have found to do the trick. How can you tell the normal ups and downs, defiant attitudes, and exaggerated acts of independence from signs that are part of the drug-using life? It isn't easy.

Most adolescents (and adults) will tell you that at one time or another they tried to get away with stealing a small item from a store, even if it was only candy from a bin at the supermarket. Most will tell you that they love to sleep late and stay up until all hours when there are no longer mandated bedtimes. Most will tell you they must talk secretly to friends on the phone. Each of these behaviors may be a "warning sign" in a certain context, but each can also be a normal part of growing up.

Because the line is so fine between expected behavior and troubling behavior, most parents, who want to think the best of their children, do not see signs of danger. But knowing what to watch out for can help you determine if your child is involved, and whether the involvement is experimental or habitual.

In general, you should suspect some drug use if you observe more than one of these indicators:

1. A change of friends from those you know to those who avoid you. (But don't pin all your youngster's troubles on "bad friends." Often the child who is already troubled is the one who is drawn to a group that is taking dangerous risks and is heavily committed to using alcohol and drugs.)
2. Friends among older teenagers and young adults. Older users need the attention and admiration they get from younger kids and often entice them to be followers and dealers.
3. A best friend who uses drugs. This is the single best indicator of use.

4. Daily cigarette smoking. This is an early warning that other substance use may be in the picture.

5. A deterioration in appearance. (The reverse is not necessarily a safety signal. Many drug users look like clean-cut all-American kids instead of the stereotypical druggie.)

6. A drop in performance at home. Chores may be neglected or done sloppily; curfews may be ignored.

7. A change in school performance. The drop in grades may not be dramatic, but watch for tardiness, truancy, and disciplinary problems.

8. Use of street or drug language.

9. Hypersensitivity, irritability. The teenage user is often hostile, avoids family contact, overreacts to mild criticism, and runs away when pressed for accountability.

10. Lack of concern about people, ideas, and values that used to be very important.

11. Wide mood swings. Although mood changes are a normal part of adolescence, extreme emotional swings can indicate a problem.

12. Secretive phone calls. Callers who hang up when you answer may be your child's new friends.

13. The disappearance of money, personal belongings, pills, or alcohol.

14. The sudden appearance of expensive merchandise. Electronic equipment, clothes, or jewelry your child can't possibly afford may indicate drug-dealing, although the teenager will probably say, "I borrowed it from a friend."

15. Lying.

16. Trouble with the law. Kids may be picked up for shoplifting, driving while intoxicated, disorderly conduct.

In addition to these general warning signals, specific drugs have specific effects. You may not see them in pure form, though, because teenagers so often use more than one drug. Also, individual reactions vary widely to any substance, whether it is marijuana, penicillin, or strawberries, depending on body chemistry. If your child is allergic to grasses, for example, his physical reactions to marijuana may be heightened. Despite these possible complications, the following case histories and charts of symptoms can alert you to the possibility that your child might be using one drug or another. The final piece of information may have to come from blood or breath testing (for alcohol) or urine testing for other drugs. Home drug-testing kits are now widely available in drugstores. Some parents, desperately concerned that their child might be a regular user, try them. If their child balks at providing a sample, they set consequences. For example, Ellen Morehouse, executive director of Student Assistance Services in New York's Westchester County, suggests that if a child has a driver's license a parent can say, "Either do the test or don't use the car." She adds, "I totally support home drug tests. Parents have to do everything in their power to keep their kids safe. They should act just as decisively as they would if they thought their child had any other life-threatening condition." Other parents are not so sure they want to force the issue in this way, and some experts feel that parents should not play detective. There is also the chance that the test may be inaccurate, since something as simple as eating poppy seeds can produce a false positive. If you decide to use a test, what's important is what you do once you know the results. If your child tests positive you should involve your pediatrician, family doctor, or other professional in finding the right help. In some cases, the test can be used to open a dialogue that had shut down before.

ALCOHOL

Alcohol is our social drug, and adults feel less threatened by it than by the other drugs, legal or illegal. Some parents say, "Thank God it's only booze." But alcohol is the drug that school and college counselors worry about the most. What's worse, alcohol combined with easily available sleeping pills or tranquilizers can lead to death. So can the combination of marijuana and alcohol. Marijuana can suppress the body's natural protection against alcohol overdose, which is vomiting. If the alcohol is not vomited up quickly enough, it can be lethal. Your teenager may say he's seen plenty of people throwing up after drinking alcohol and smoking pot. The point is not that suppression of nausea happens every time, but that it can happen unexpectedly and dangerously. Alcohol is hazardous enough even when it is used by an experienced drinker.

Alcohol

What a Parent Might See or Hear

Early Signs and Symptoms		Later Signs and Symptoms	
Physical	*Behavioral*	*Physical*	*Behavioral*
Red eyes	Pre-party	Shakes when	Excessive
Headaches	drinking	not drinking	sleeping
(i.e., hang-	Sneaking	Tolerance:	Fights/
overs)	drinks	needing	arguments

Lack of coordination

Unsteady gait

Drowsiness

Alcohol on breath

Blackouts (memory loss)

Slurred speech

more or a lot to get drunk

Physical illnesses: liver and cardiac damage reported by physician

Solitary drinking

Dropping of nondrinking friends

Falls

Burns

Bruises

Use of alcohol to calm down

Lack of control, saying unexpected things

Marny started drinking heavily when she was only thirteen. Before then she had been close to her parents. When she began to change physically, she began to change emotionally, too, avoiding confidences and physical contact. One night she sneaked into the house after a friend's birthday party, ran upstairs, closed her door, and yelled down that she was too tired for a goodnight kiss. Her parents chalked it up to "maturing."

But her father now says, "That's when we should have caught it. She didn't want us to smell her breath." Marny began to drink every weekend. She says, "I would guzzle a quart of vodka at a time. I could have gotten the money, but I had a friend whose parents didn't watch their liquor closet."

She tried outpatient treatment, but after about eight months began staying out late again, was grounded for a month, forged a note to get out of school, and was caught.

Only when she started coming home so drunk she couldn't climb the stairs did her family agree that an inpatient program was needed. She is now recovering.

PILLS

Young people become addicted to pills through a variety of routes. Some come across them by chance in a parent's medicine chest, others buy them on the street or from friends and quickly enjoy the high. And some become victims of a pusher who says, "Try these, you'll like them." Among the most commonly used are amphetamines (uppers or diet pills) and barbiturates (downers).

AMPHETAMINES

At first Cindy was given pills by her mother. She says, "My favorite drug was speed. My mother was always on my case about overeating, so when I was eleven, she gave me pills to control my weight. I took them for that and because they made me feel good. At sixteen or seventeen I started on alcohol to calm down when I was jittery, but I kept taking other things, too. I'd forget to come home, I wouldn't call because I thought they'd know I was high, and I got really paranoid. I thought my father was following me. I could have had an accident because I kept looking in the rearview mirror while I was driving. I wish my parents had done something to get me help before they did. They knew—I'm sure they knew."

Amphetamines			
What a Parent Might See or Hear			
Early Signs and Symptoms		**Later Signs and Symptoms**	
Physical	*Behavioral*	*Physical*	*Behavioral*
Pupils dilated	Increased alertness	Fever	Psychosis (i.e., seeing, hearing, believing things that are not there)
	Frenetic behavior	Sweating	
	Restlessness	Rashes	
	Talkativeness	Increased susceptibility to illness	
	Excitement	Complaints about headache, vision	Sleeplessness
	Hostility, suspicion		Hallucinations
	Irritability		Bizarre behavior
			Paranoia

BARBITURATES

Phil got his first pills when he had a part-time job at a drugstore. He was always a good student and a talented musician. Then he started coming home with headaches, and his grades slipped. His mother says, "We didn't realize what was happening until I found some pills, downers, in his room. He said he got them out of the garbage pail at work. We tried to find out why he was doing it, but he gave us the silent treatment. We made him quit his job, but it didn't help." Then he began coming into the house in a disoriented state and falling asleep in the daytime. He even slept through Thanksgiving at his grandmother's house.

Now he's quit school, is living on his own, and is resisting any attempt to get him into treatment.

Barbiturates			
What a Parent Might See or Hear			
Early Signs and Symptoms		**Later Signs and Symptoms**	
Physical	*Behavioral*	*Physical*	*Behavioral*
Slow breathing	Slow speech, disorientation, behavior that looks like drunkenness, but with no odor of alcohol	Circulatory problems	Constant grogginess
Headaches	Deficiency in thinking	Malnourishment— emaciation	Paranoid delusions
	Sluggishness	Decayed teeth	Seeking amphetamines to counter drug effects
	Moodiness		Loss of appetite
	Faulty judgment		
	Falling asleep while reading, etc.		

INHALANTS

Children as young as eight years old inhale household products to get high. They are not properly "drugs," but volatile chemicals that are not meant for human consumption. The most popular are spray paints and gasoline, but kids also use such easily available substances as correction fluid, marking pens, glue, and lighter fluid. Use peaks at about the age of fourteen and then drops off with or without intervention when youngsters have more access to and interest in "real drugs." The poisonous fumes are sniffed (sometimes directly from the container), snorted, bagged (inhaled from a plastic bag placed over the face or head and sometimes fastened with a clothespin), or huffed (from a plastic bag or such things as an inhalant-soaked rag, sock, or toilet paper roll stuffed into the mouth). Children are taught the routine by other children. The giveaway may be a strange chemical smell or stains on the fingers. The initial effects are usually fast to come and fast to go, so children can sniff in school between classes, on the school bus, or in their rooms and then, a few minutes later, seem perfectly normal.

Prolonged or frequent use is another matter. Far from being an innocent childish amusement, inhalant use can cause oxygen deprivation, serious damage to the brain, heart, liver, lungs and kidneys, and even death. Between five hundred and six hundred young users a year die.

Bob's parents knew something was wrong when he dropped his hobbies, changed friends, and became a loner. He seemed to have insomnia, getting up late at night to wander around the house. They took him first to a school counselor who said nothing was wrong, then to a drug treatment center for evaluation. His urine test was negative.

Still struggling to help him, they missed the evidence that was right under their eyes—cans of spray paint. He was a bike racer, and he had brought his bike into his bedroom and suddenly started repainting it every week. His night-time activity was huffing the fumes from a plastic bag. They found him one morning next to his bicycle with a spray can in his hand—dead.

Inhalants			
What a Parent Might See or Hear			
Early Signs and Symptoms		**Later Signs and Symptoms**	
Physical	*Behavioral*	*Physical*	*Behavioral*
Nausea	Giddiness	Memory loss	Occasional angry
Blurred	Staggering	Brain damage	outbursts
vision		Unconscious-	Change in
Headaches		ness (may	coordination
Stains on		occur with	
fingers		only one use)	
Strange			
smell			

MARIJUANA

Since marijuana stays in the body for weeks or even much longer, your child may be somewhat stoned all the time even if he or she is just an occasional or weekend user. This makes it hard to assess what is and what isn't change in be-havior—you may never see the child really free of the drug.

Nevertheless, you can learn to recognize some clear-cut indicators. One way to check out your suspicions right after
you think your child has smoked a joint is to smell your
child's fingers for the telltale acrid odor.

Marijuana			
What a Parent Might See or Hear			
Early Signs and Symptoms		**Later Signs and Symptoms**	
Physical	*Behavioral*	*Physical*	*Behavioral*
Red eyes	Lack of mo-tivation	Loss of timing (e.g., trouble hitting or catching a ball)	Slowed normal functioning (may look like laziness)
Fatigue	Lethargy; "doesn't care"		
Apathy			
Hunger			
Cough			
Chest pains	Changes in grooming	Poor short-term memory	Lack of emotional growth to-ward matur-ity, inability to take responsibility
	Mood swings	Irregular men-strual cycles	
	Irritability	Increased number of physical illnesses	
	Increased friction with family, peers		Withdrawal
			Highway accidents
	Difficulty concentrat-ing; grades slipping	Impaired motor skills	
		Distorted sense of time, distance	

Cora's mother always dropped her off at high school on her way to work. She didn't realize that school didn't start for an hour and that Cora, who was fourteen, spent the time smoking cigarettes and pot with friends. Then she got a call from the school nurse: "Cora is sitting here with me. She seems groggy. Her teacher says she was giggling in class and then went to sleep at her desk. Has she been sick?" That was when Cora's mother remembered that it was difficult to get her attention, and that she sometimes just sat on the living-room couch and stared into space. She'd been wearing dark glasses in the house, too. It finally dawned on the mother that her daughter was smoking marijuana.

COCAINE

Cocaine use, even a single experiment, can be lethal. It can cause sudden heart irregularities, heart attacks, and convulsions in otherwise healthy young people. Like other drugs, cocaine also affects the unborn fetus. Hospitals are seeing large numbers of young cocaine-using mothers whose babies are born prematurely, with birth defects or low birth weight. The drug has only belatedly been recognized as the killer that it is.

Seventeen-year-old Craig left a picnic after snorting cocaine all evening. When he drove his girlfriend home, he grazed a tree planted, as he insisted later, "too close to the curb." Craig stopped at a gas station to get the bent left rearview mirror straightened and the attendant asked, "What's happened to your elbow?" He twisted his left arm around and stared at the torn sweatshirt and the bleeding flesh. He hadn't felt a thing because of the anesthetic action of the drug.

Craig's life deteriorated after the accident as he began using more cocaine and followed it with alcohol to calm down. He felt like Superman one minute and down in the dumps the next. He became suspicious and depressed, and finally was snorting every day. In school he missed classes, was warned about failing, and got so angry at his math teacher that he punched a desk and broke a bone in his hand. But his parents became concerned only when they noticed how unnaturally thin he had become. By then he was so out of control, frightened, and depressed that he was thinking about suicide.

Cocaine

What a Parent Might See or Hear

Early Signs and Symptoms		Later Signs and Symptoms	
Physical	*Behavioral*	*Physical*	*Behavioral*
Dialated pupils	Rapid mood	Chronic cough	Memory
Runny nose	changes,	Constipation	problems
Hoarse voice	ups and	Sore throat	Violence
Increased sen-	downs	Black or gray	Paranoia
sory awareness	Unexplained	sputum	Depression
(ordinary	anger and	Exhaustion	Suicide
lightbulb	edginess	Nasal bleeding	attempt
may be	Reversal of	Convulsions	
blinding)	day/night	Weight loss	
Pallor	cycle	Tooth decay	
Profuse			
sweating			

LSD

After its popularity in the sixties as the "hippie drug" and a carryover of that trend into the seventies, LSD use declined. In the 1990s it is back as the favorite hallucinogen of teenagers. It produces enhanced sensory effects and is a potent mood-changer. Called "acid," it is often imprinted on colorful blotter sheets with pictures of teen favorites such as Bart Simpson, teddy bears, and peace signs. The drug can be licked off these sheets, or swallowed in capsule, tablets, or liquid form. Its use can result in bizarre behavior and even tragic reactions such as psychotic episodes and suicide. "Flashbacks" can occur even after use has stopped.

One young man was persuaded by his girlfriend, who had used the drug before, to try it and experience the sensory changes she was so enthusiastic about. They took it together. Within a few minutes he was on the floor, his movements becoming slower and slower. Finally, he stopped moving altogether and she could not get him to respond. In a panic, she called three friends. They came quickly and together they decided not to get him to a hospital because they were afraid he would "freak out" if he regained consciousness in those surroundings. For six hours, they watched his breathing and his skin color. Suddenly he woke up, said, "Is that all there is?" and began sobbing. They were all so shaken by the experience that none of them used LSD after that. Some experts speculate that the drop in use that occurred in the 1980s can be traced to the bad experiences young people witnessed. Today, teenagers have never seen what can happen during a "bad trip" and are less aware of the dangers of using the drug.

LSD (ACID)

What a Parent Might See or Hear

Signs and Symptoms

Physical	*Behavioral*	*"Bad Trip"*
Rapid heart rate	Insomnia	Extreme anxiety
Dilated pupils	Extreme sensitivity	Panic
Fever	to stimuli	Rapid mood swings
Sweating	Uncontrollable	Confusion
Loss of appetite	laughing	Psychotic episodes
		Unusual sense of
		power

TELLING USE FROM ABUSE

Although it's not always easy to distinguish between drug use and abuse, in young children any use is abuse and should be taken seriously. The same is true of junior high students, although the one-time experiment with beer is not necessarily a sign of worse things to come. However, if drinking or smoking marijuana is a regular part of social life in junior high, this is a sign of trouble. One drug counselor has this rule of thumb: "Three tries is experimentation. More than that is use."

Statistically speaking, the occasional social use of alcohol and marijuana is "normal" in the later years of high school, but here, too, you have to make an individual judgment. If a child seventeen or eighteen years old smokes pot at a party once a month, maintains good grades, and gets along well at home and with friends, you can and should express concern about the risks of such behavior, but the child is not an addict.

A Washington, D.C., drug counselor developed her own simple scale for assessing where a child fits on the continuum of use and abuse. "If a kid goes outside with friends after school to smoke and then goes home, that's use," she decided. "It becomes abuse if he uses after school, goes home, then goes out again to use. It is addiction if he uses before school, at his lunch break, after school, and in the evening—if he has to have it."

More formally, the steps toward addiction have been characterized as:

1. Exploration. Teenagers are curious about the world around them. They also go to great lengths to avoid being called a nerd, so they give it a try.
2. Learning the mood swing. If they use more regularly, they soon know what it feels like to be high.
3. Seeking the mood swing. The child is attached to a feeling he can count on rather than the particular drug. Use escalates to the point where he may be using at weekend-long parties as well as hoarding a supply at home.
4. Preoccupation with getting the drug and getting high. Youngsters drink to get drunk rather than to have a good time, moving from anticipation to obsession. They plan when, where, and how to use the substance. Finally, they may use it alone, in their rooms, "and that's the loneliest feeling of all," says one boy.
5. Needing the substance to feel normal. This is chemical dependency.

Adolescents tend to develop addiction more rapidly than adults. Some teenagers become alcoholics within six months of their first drink. Not every young person who drinks heavily, though, is going to become dependent on alcohol. Studies show that as they get older, their drinking often drops off. Marriage is the great stabilizer, and tends to lower drug use as well as drinking.

Many myths surround the definition of addiction. A few years ago, only those drugs that frequently produce physical dependence—heroin, sedatives, alcohol, and cigarettes—were considered addictive. People could say, "I don't use every day. I don't get withdrawal symptoms when I stop," and convince themselves and those around them that they were not hooked. But now doctors emphasize psychological and behavioral patterns in their definition, even without physical dependence. These patterns include:

- Loss of control
- Craving and compulsion
- Continued use, despite physical and behavioral problems or a wish to stop
- A tendency to deny that a drug problem exists

Says Dr. Arnold Washton, cofounder of the 800-COCAINE Hotline, "If they're hungover in school, their girlfriend or boyfriend is worried, their parents are angry, and they still want to maintain they're not addicted . . . they're in trouble."

Parents' responses can be a barometer of a child's problem with drugs. Dr. Donald Ian MacDonald, formerly head of the Alcohol, Drug Abuse and Mental Health Administration and father of a boy who went through drug abuse treatment, says, "I ask the mother when she last had a good night's sleep, and if she starts crying, I know her kid is in difficulty."

FACING SUICIDE

It may seem strange to find a section on suicide in a book about drug use and abuse. But the fact is that alcohol and drugs are part of the picture in almost half the cases of young people who kill themselves and often a factor in attempted suicides as well. Drugs cloud judgment and deepen sad feelings. But finding drugs and alcohol in the life histories of young suicides doesn't mean that drugs took a healthy kid and made him suicidal. It probably means he was unhappy to begin with and took drugs or alcohol in order to feel better.

Four young people—two boys and two girls—who died of carbon monoxide poisoning in a rare suicide pact in Bergenfield, New Jersey, had cocaine in their bloodstreams. The two boys, who had started drinking again after treatment for alcohol abuse, were legally drunk at the time of their deaths. The father of one of the boys said he believed his son would never have killed himself if he had been sober.

For parents who already feel they have lost their drug-abusing children to an alien world, deaths like these intensify the ever-present fear that their own children will make an irrevocable decision and leave the real world forever. It makes sense for you to be aware of the warning signs so that you can anticipate a suicidal act.

Most young people who take their own lives give warning signs. Some of them are the same warnings as for drug abuse—others are more specific.

DANGER SIGNS

- A change in sleeping habits. The child may be unable to sleep or sleep a lot more than usual.
- A change in eating habits.
- Isolation. The child may spend hours alone and stay away from friends.
- A preoccupation with death. The child may show intense interest in art and music that deal with death.
- A previous suicide attempt. Don't say, "He was only trying to get attention." Most people who succeed in taking their own lives have made a previous attempt.
- Changes in dress and grooming. When a stylish dresser starts looking scruffy or a boy who took long showers every day starts smelling like a locker room, pay attention.
- Changes in mood and behavior. Adolescents often go from high to low within minutes, and it's hard to know what is significant and what isn't. But if there is a sudden change from sullen and subdued to exuberant or from outgoing to secretive, be wary.

CRISIS SIGNS

Get help immediately if your child:

- Becomes suddenly cheerful and calm after a depression. This may indicate that the internal conflict is over and that a decision to die has been made.
- Gives away treasured possessions. "My son started to clean up his room and give things away—his guitar, his

old tapes. I hadn't seen the floor of his room for months and suddenly it was almost bare," says the mother of a son who made a serious suicide attempt.

- Uses the past tense when talking about life. "You've been a good father"; "I always loved you."

A social worker with a decade of experience working with troubled youngsters suggests that if your child expresses the feeling that "It's not worth it," you should ask directly, "Are you feeling so bad that you want to hurt yourself?" She adds, "You should not leave a child who seems imminently suicidal alone."

Not all youngsters who show one or more of these signs are suicidal, and not all who don't are safe. One mother says, "If he had only looked worse, we might have suspected. But he seemed fine." External factors not on these lists can complicate things, too. If someone else in the family, or a friend or a classmate, has committed suicide, the risk is increased. Susan White-Bowden, whose son killed himself two years after his father took his own life, says in her book *Everything to Live For* that one of her mistakes was not saying to her children, "What your father did was wrong, and it was bad." So her son "looked up to what his father had done." In a similar vein, experts on teen suicide warn that schools should not romanticize it by naming an auditorium or putting up a plaque for a youngster who killed himself. To protect the other children, they say, you have to get the message across that "suicide is not romantic or heroic, but stupid."

News stories or TV movies on suicides are also possible influences. A study of teen suicides found that deaths increased in the week after network TV shows reported such tragedies. People who specialize in the study of suicide also caution that spring and the period just after the Christmas holidays are particularly sensitive seasons, as are the times when a revered teacher leaves or a valued friend moves away.

Even without any of these factors, if you notice that your youngster shows any signs that make you uneasy, trust your intuition that something bad might happen. A suicide threat should be taken seriously. It may be straightforward—"I'm going to blow my brains out"—or it may be more subtle—"Nothing is any use—it doesn't matter"; "Maybe I won't be around tomorrow"; "Nobody cares." Don't jump on the youngster with "You don't mean that" or "Don't talk that way." It's frightening and upsetting to hear your child say that whatever you've tried isn't enough and that his or her life isn't worth much. But dismissing the expression of these feelings is dangerous and only intensifies the youngster's distress.

Young people consider killing themselves for three reasons, according to Dr. James Egan, a child psychiatrist associated with the Children's National Medical Center in Washington, D.C.: a real wish to die; a wish for rebirth or joining with someone who is dead; or a wish to call attention to themselves, a desperate situation, or the plight of another person, not really a wish to die.

In another study, Dr. Michael L. Peck and Dr. Robert Litman, while with the Suicide Prevention Center in Los Angeles, looked at why youngsters try to commit suicide, and found that they see their feelings of unhappiness, frustration, or failure as unacceptable to their parents. When they try to tell their parents how they feel, the parents ignore them, deny that things are that bad, or become hostile.

A better approach would be to adopt the suggestions of

Dr. Edward Schneidman, a pioneer in suicide prevention research. These guidelines were developed for counselors, but their commonsense advice can be useful for parents, too.

First, don't try to cheer suicidal people up or provide false reassurance. Make it clear that you take their feelings seriously and tell them you will try to help them deal with their complaints.

Second, make a list of alternatives to suicide. Discuss each item listed. A person who is considering suicide can't conceive of alternative ways out. He feels that all the doors are closed, and you have to show him one that is open. Even a small glimmer of hope that things can be better, that someone hears his cry and will help, can make a difference. You may have to act as a container for angry feelings, but try to be a ceramic-lined container that doesn't get scarred by acid. Therapists who work with suicidal youths say that they are often ambivalent about dying and expect to be rescued. They aren't really trying to kill themselves—they are trying to kill the pain that makes life unbearable. If you can reduce the pain by listening and providing alternatives, you can reduce the risk.

If your child does threaten suicide or actually succeeds, no one can say with any certainty, "It's all because the kid was on drugs," or "The parents didn't care enough." It isn't that clear. Some human beings are more able than others to withstand the wounds of life. They seem to have been born that way. In addition, some maturational turning points seem to be more stressful than others. As many teenagers see it, you only get one chance. Blow this one, and it's over. Every hurt, every defeat, is final.

Other youngsters seem to have a built-in ability to weather life's crises. The vulnerable ones, faced with the same circumstances, see no way out. "Life seems an endless, bleak present, with no hope of change to the depressed," says Dr. Herbert Rappaport, a psychologist at Temple University who has studied how time perception affects people's lives. Drug addicts, too, feel hopeless about the future. "Drug use," he explains, "is a way to intensify the present and ignore the future."

IN THE BEGINNING

Cigarettes, alcohol, and marijuana are seen as "gateway drugs," opening the door for the use of other drugs. The sixth-grader who smokes cigarettes (smoking has to be learned) or drinks may be on his way. The earlier and more intense the commitment in these initial stages, the greater the chance it will continue to a later stage or start again after a pause. One survey of youngsters in grades six to twelve published in the *Journal of School Health* found that daily cigarette smoking is the best statistical predictor of future trouble. The "gateway" theory has been disputed by some experts as simply the observation of a statistical progression, but new studies show that nicotine, alcohol, and marijuana trigger the same pleasurable pathways in the brain as cocaine, amphetamines, and heroin. Regular, heavy use may prime the brain to seek out the more powerful drugs.

The progression, according to Dr. Denise Kandel of Columbia University, often goes from beer and wine to cigarettes or hard liquor, then on to marijuana and finally to other illicit drugs. A stage that involves misuses of prescription drugs or heavy drinking may precede use of illicit drugs. "Crack" is a special case. Youths who have little or no experience with other drugs have been turning to it. According to Dr. Arnold Washton, "This is the first drug they get involved with and within days or weeks they find they are strapped with a full-blown addiction."

The usual sequence doesn't mean that every child who smokes cigarettes will inevitably go on to use illicit drugs. It means only that he or she is more likely to move on to other substances in this order, and that a parent should be aware of that possibility. Also, the harsh reality is that as time goes on, a child is likely to add the use of one drug to use of another.

The pattern of alcohol use is a good clue to "polydrug" use. Dr. Elizabeth Morrisey, who was at the University of Washington when she surveyed almost fifteen hundred adolescents, says, "If a youngster is asked how much he or she drank on one occasion in the last month, and the answer is, say, ten or more drinks, then for sure he or she is a multiple drug user." The majority of such children used marijuana and amphetamines in addition to alcohol.

While multiple drug use is predicted by alcohol use, the single best predictor of who will use cocaine is who has used marijuana one hundred times or more, according to Dr. Carleton Turner, former assistant to President Reagan for drug abuse policy. In other words, familiarity with one drug may prepare the way for use of others.

WHERE TO LOOK AND WHAT TO LOOK FOR

Some drugs leave an open trail. Cigarette smoke settles in hair, in clothes, and on fingertips, where a parent can smell the evidence. Inhalants often have a peculiar odor, and the containers from which they came are easy to identify. But other drug use is harder to detect.

Parents are understandably reluctant to invade a child's private space to search for evidence, fearing they will do serious damage to their relationship. But one worried mother steeled herself to read the diary her daughter had left out on her bed. She was shocked by the sexual adventures, but relieved that her daughter had resisted efforts to get her to try "crystal meth," an amphetamine derivative. The mother says, "I decided to risk having Kathy furious with me for a while, hoping she would eventually learn to trust me again." Kathy stormed out of the house and stayed overnight with a friend. "It was the hardest night of my life," her mother says. "But then she came back and we talked. She finally admitted that it was a relief that I knew what had been going on. Now she doesn't have to lie anymore, and I don't have to wonder what she's hiding."

If you've done everything and still feel you need to go on a search, try to get your child to join you. Surprisingly, as the head of a chemical dependency unit says, "Most times the child will give you the drugs and then the conversation can center on solutions."

Not every child reacts in this way, however, and drug users are as ingenious as squirrels in hiding their hoard. If you have to search on your own, a police department Youth Squad detective suggests you look first in the obvious places—a workshop or garage where the youngster spends a lot of time, a rec room or the basement, and of course the child's room. Check your kid's closet or dresser. Extra shoes are a good hiding place; so are jacket pockets and under clothing in the backs of drawers. The stuff may even be hidden in your room, since it is most unlikely you would search there. "Usually," the detective says, "it's in a spot the parents walk around often."

More unusual containers for alcohol and other drugs include stereo speakers, hardbound books that have a hole cut in the pages, stuffed animals, air-conditioner vents, freezers, and "stash cans," which look like ordinary soft-drink containers but have removable tops and are designed to hide drugs.

Parents can also get a hint about drug usage by paying careful attention to the inscriptions on camp pictures, in yearbooks, and on school programs from dances, plays, and athletic events. What your child's friends think is noteworthy can alert you to what has been happening. One girl's yearbook picture was inscribed: "Remember me and all the times we got stoned together."

The presence of incense, magazines such as *High Times*, and drug paraphernalia almost certainly are tip-offs. Strange-looking glass shapes may be bongs for smoking marijuana. Small pipes can be used for crack. Small pieces of screen or sink faucet sieves or bits of scouring pads can be used in homemade pipes. Cigars can be hollowed out and filled with marijuana to make "blunts," a new favorite. One mother found a razor blade stuck in a candle in her son's room and learned later that the blade was a standard tool for cutting clumps of cocaine and placing the powder into lines to be sniffed.

If you find seeds, powder, or pills you can't identify, or something you think might be used to take a drug, you might take it to your local police department or youth bureau. Many of them can do simple tests immediately, or they can send the substance away to be analyzed. Policemen and counselors who work with youngsters can also often identify the more common paraphernalia by sight.

The naivete of parents can be astounding, whether they are faced with unfamiliar paraphernalia, physical symptoms, or the evidence of their own eyes. Parents even miss signals the kids themselves are trying to give them. "He was trying to give us a message," says the mother of a boy who used everything from alcohol to LSD. He told his parents to watch a TV movie about a girl who was addicted to drugs, swore again and again to stop, and finally died. They wondered why he was so insistent, but didn't connect those events with his experiences. Now that he's been in treatment, they know—"That was his life, too."

THE RUNAWAYS

When a child runs away, it is like a punch in the nose, a shocking message that says, "You're such a lousy parent, I don't even want to live with you." The child perceives the world away from home as a source of freedom, a carefree playground. Yet most teenagers who run away stay close to home and come back on their own.

The first time one boy ran away was "when he was eight years old. We found him hours later in a neighbor's backyard," his mother remembers. When he was a teenager, he climbed out a window and took off with two drug-using friends. That night he'd rebelled against his curfew and shouted, "I'm not going to live by your rules." Many of the warning signs that a child may run away are the same as those of drug use, and the two often go together.

"We didn't recognize the running away as a message," says his mother. "But we should have known then that he wasn't just smoking pot occasionally as we thought."

What should you do if your child runs away and does not come back promptly? After you have checked with friends, neighbors, and relatives, a private detective with experience in tracing missing persons suggests that you:

- Report the child missing to the police.
- Provide a recent photo, names of his friends and relatives, and a list of his favorite activities.
- Make an inventory of things he may have taken with him, such as clothing, a bank account book, charge account cards, credit cards, or articles of value.
- Check the youngster's correspondence for leads.

It is important that you use any opening, such as a phone call from the child, or from a friend, or from a staff member at a shelter, to persuade your child to come home voluntarily. The runaway who is most likely to harbor long-lasting resentments and to run away again is the one who is picked up by the police and forcibly returned home.

Chronic runaways are a special problem. If they are involved with drugs or alcohol, they are not only frightened, confused, and guilt-ridden, but they get to the point where they can no longer face their parents, and they "split." Some go so far as to contemplate suicide. Some of the families of these youngsters have set impossibly high standards without helping their children achieve the independence and maturity they need. Sometimes the children have been subjected to physical or sexual abuse and are particularly vulnerable to pimps and others who appear to offer protection or affection.

One runaway, sixteen-year-old Polly, had been in and out of counseling for two years. She would smoke pot, feel ashamed, and go back into treatment. But sometimes she felt like such a failure she simply got stoned and hit the road. Her parents were frantic. They wouldn't leave the apartment for fear Polly might call or the police might arrive with bad news.

One time Polly ran away and called her parents for money for a plane ticket. They were so relieved, they sent the money immediately, but instead of coming home she used it to buy more drugs. Finally she ended up in jail. That time her parents let her spend two days and nights there. Then they sent her a prepaid, nonredeemable bus ticket, and Polly arrived home. Despite the chance that you will be conned, it would be foolhardy of you to ignore your child's pleas. With help from the police, social service agencies, and a ticket—no money—you have a way and some power to get your child home.

If you hear nothing and searching does not help, all you can do is hope. Sometimes distance and time can help a child rediscover the strength of family ties and come home. When your runaway does return, it may be hard for all of you to talk about what has just happened. Sometimes a cooling-off period with the child staying someplace else for a while can provide healing time. Later, you can start to deal with the drug abuse and other problems that the running away signaled so vividly.

PART 2

What to Do

4

Talking and Listening: The Two-Way Street

My father said I could always talk to him. I was eight years old and I said I got a D in conduct. He beat the hell out of me. What I learned was not to believe him.

—DEACON FARRELL J. HOPKINS, ARCHDIOCESE OF NEW YORK

Talking to your children is only half the communication story. Listening is the other half. Everyone needs to be listened to, but adolescents who are changing, searching for an identity, and looking for answers need an attentive audience more than most. You play a big part. If you are committed to listening, you have to stop what you are doing (put the newspaper down, turn off the TV, lay aside the salad-making) and take what is said seriously. What you say in response is important, too. Your child may be accustomed to your offering advice, but that could be the last thing he is looking for. Nor does he want you to top his

81

story by telling one of your own. What you want to achieve is a kind of mutual respect, the same kind you would give to or expect from a close friend.

This is not easy. Some children set themselves up so that no one hears what they are saying. Some kids complain so consistently that they are ignored because of the monotony. Others screech, so they are simply asked to quiet down. One boy, when asked how a movie was, would give a frame-by-frame description of the production, making it hard for anyone to pay attention to him after a while. Another bristled when asked any questions, treating even the most innocent request for information as an invasion of privacy.

Despite such difficulties as these, the important thing is to keep listening—and keep talking. It may be necessary to go through stormy times before reaching the calm that often comes after the age of twenty. If your child is still an adolescent or younger, these dos and don'ts may help you both navigate through the turbulence.

DO LISTEN TO YOUR CHILD

Sometimes listening to your child is as simple as keeping quiet for a few minutes. One mother imagines her lips sealed with masking tape—straight across for some topics, just partly sealed for topics on which some comment might be appropriate.

Sometimes "active" listening is required. This technique, described in the book *Parent Effectiveness Training* by Dr. Thomas Gordon, involves reflecting the underlying meaning of what the child is saying. For example, a teenage girl comes home from school and says to her mother, "I have nothing to wear. Everything around here's a mess." A tuned-in parent might respond, "You sound angry. What happened at school today?"

Done too often, this can be annoying, or can sound as if you are talking down. But done well, it can help bring feelings out into the open and assure the young person that he or she is being appreciated and understood.

DO LISTEN FOR WHAT IS NOT SAID

When your child tells you about a friend who is getting into trouble or having a hard time keeping up with schoolwork, be alert to the possibility that the difficulties may be closer to home.

DO LISTEN TO YOURSELF

Listen to your tone of voice, how you talk, and what you say. Do you always sound annoyed, rushed, or disapproving? Do you run the same tape over and over? "There goes Dad again with that old story about making the touchdown in the big game" is likely to be the reaction, with a firm closing of the ears to what you thought would be interesting.

DO LISTEN TO THE WAY YOU AND YOUR SPOUSE TALK TO EACH OTHER

Some parents say no more than "What's for dinner?" in front of their children, or they communicate in angry bursts. You can't provide such a model and expect to see a much different style in your youngsters.

DO SPEND LISTENING TIME WITH EACH CHILD EACH DAY

Ten minutes along doing what the child wants to do during the evening, after school, or even before school in the morning provides time for talking without interruption. If you start this habit when your children are young, you can ease communication when the need for adolescent privacy comes along. On the other hand, it's never too late to start.

DO TIME YOUR TALKS

No one communicates on command, particularly not a teenager, whose automatic response is likely to range from cautiousness to a firmly sealed mouth. It's important to talk on the child's schedule. If he says, "I'd like to talk," in an ideal situation you would drop whatever it is you have to do, sit in a quiet place, and listen. (The child may never bring the subject up again if you say, "Not now. I'm busy.") In real life, however, it's not always possible to stop everything and pay attention. At times like that you can explain why you can't talk ("I'd like to, Tim, but I have to get to work") and then set a specific time ("How about six o'clock tonight?") when the two of you can get together. Try not to evade the situation or your responsibility by saying, "Go talk to your father."

A parent also has to learn to be sensitive to the unsaid "I want to talk to you" clues that a child may provide. A youngster who follows you around the house without saying anything, who hovers over you as you prepare dinner, who remains behind when the others leave the house, may be signaling that he has something he wants to say. One way to push the door open wider might be to express what you sense: "I have the feeling there's something on your mind. Do you want to talk about it?"

DO PREPARE YOURSELF

When a talk has been planned or concerns a sensitive subject, it is not something you can just stumble into; prepare yourself to deal with the inevitable tension by reviewing your convictions, redefining family goals in your own head, and thinking in terms of age-appropriate information for your child. Keep in mind his sensitivities, what he does and does not know, and what puzzles him.

DO MEAN WHAT YOU SAY

There are parents who can't say no decisively. Their resolve falters after a while. "Can I have the car, Dad?" "No." And a few minutes later, "Oh, please, Dad, can't I have the car?" "No." And then again, "Can't I have the car, Dad?" "Oh, all right. Go ahead." It's all right to change your mind, but let the child know why and stick by your decision if you feel it is important, no matter how much you are pushed. Don't be like the bumper sticker that says, "Maybe. And that's final."

DO GIVE COMPLIMENTS AND HUGS AS WELL AS CRITICISM

In some families down through the generations, praise has been avoided as a corrupter of the young—and even the old.

An eighty-year-old woman refrained from telling her sixty-year-old daughter how nice she looked because "I don't want to spoil her."

A child who is greeted every day with something like "Go clean up your room" or "Your hair is a mess—you can't go to school like that" won't feel very good. Children—at least young ones—believe what their parents say. So genuine praise and emotional and physical warmth go a long way toward building a healthy self-image. Compliments are food for growth. That doesn't mean they should come pouring out, particularly if they are not warranted, but a parent can look for a child's strengths and give credit—"We're proud of the way you're doing your homework before you go out"; "You were great in the game today"; "We loved the cookies you baked."

DO REVIVE THE OLD CUSTOM OF FAMILY MEALS

In some families, eating together has gone out of style. Stand-up snacks have replaced sit-down dinners. Yet mealtime offers a wonderful chance to listen to children, to let them know how you feel, and to let them learn to respect one another. Set specific times for meals, even if it is only once or twice a week, so that everyone's activities can be geared to that schedule. One family holds a traditional Sunday noontime lunch during which each child can bring up a complaint, tell about a triumph, report on the week's events, or make requests. The parents have the same privileges.

DON'T FREEZE UP OR DEFLECT UNCOMFORTABLE TOPICS

Let your children tell you their opinions on politics or their attitudes on sexual responsibility, and listen respectfully, even if you disagree. (When more than six hundred boys and girls aged fifteen to eighteen were asked how open they could be about sex in talking with their parents, 55 percent said they couldn't talk about it at all, and that their parents responded with "I'm too busy," teasing, or getting annoyed.) Help your kids to realize that they can talk about things that make them—or you—angry, confused, ashamed, or afraid. Let them know that you understand their feelings.

DON'T GIVE LECTURES

Sentences that start with "When I was a kid we never . . ." or "In our family we don't . . ." will never lead to confidences. An air of self-righteousness is usually a turn-off.

DON'T USE RIDICULE

The clothes, music, and language youngsters are attached to may seem bizarre to you, but for children (and adults, too) they are an important part of "belonging."

A consciousness of what's "in" begins very early. One six-year-old girl, just starting first grade, had never worn dresses before. The girls in her class dressed up for school. She insisted on doing the same, and the frillier the dress, the better. Making fun of her newly found way of relating to friends would have made her feel uncomfortable both at home and at school.

DON'T OVERREACT

Your children have lived with you since they were born. They know you. They know what to say to make you lose your temper. And they also know how to placate you. Surprise them by not jumping on cue, while remembering that they will try out with words things they have never done and never intend to do. One twelve-year-old boy asked his father if he could "borrow" the pistol his father had brought back as a souvenir from the Vietnam War. The boy knew he was treading on holy territory, but he wanted to test the limits of the forbidden. He also enjoyed imagining the interest and admiration he would arouse in his friends when he arrived with the prize at a neighborhood sleep-over. His father's simple "no" was not only the expected response but also the accepted one.

HOW TO TALK ABOUT DRUGS AND ALCOHOL

Most parents have not practiced talking to their children about touchy subjects, and the use of alcohol, tobacco, and drugs is among the touchiest. It's easy to talk about the weather. It's easy to talk about the home team. It's even easy to talk about taking turns or caring for pets. But when parents and children come to talk to one another about emotionally charged subjects, it is not easy at all. The awkwardness inherent in these situations was highlighted in the recent movie *The Ice Storm*, when a father tells his teenage son, "If you're worried about anything at all, just feel free to ask. And we'll, uh, look it up." Parents are so uncomfortable with the subject of drugs, according to Dr.

Lloyd D. Johnston, director of the University of Michigan's Monitoring the Future study, that they are even less likely to talk about the problem now than in the past.

The whole family must understand that drinking, smoking, using drugs, and many other adolescent behaviors are subjects for discussion, not confrontation, and, above all, they are not to be hidden. Families must also understand that, in the words of Dr. Kenneth Schonberg, director of the division of adolescent medicine at Montefiore Hospital in New York, "it is the inalienable right of parents to worry about their children."

This concern plays a part in blocking forthright communication. Fear is often disguised as anger and is expressed at full volume, shutting off any potential dialogue. One mother recalled the time her child ran out into the street. She was terrified, but her first reaction was unadulterated fury, and she immediately hit the child in response to her own fear. A few minutes later there were hugs and tears all around.

Another thing that shuts off dialogue is giving mixed messages. One drug counselor says that when she was growing up her parents told her, "You can talk to us about anything," then added by their unspoken attitudes, "But don't tell us you're pregnant and don't tell us you're using drugs."

Communication quickly shuts down under other circumstances, too. Sarcasm is a sure block. "Don't try to fool me—I know what you're up to" will put a halt to conversation. So will playing the martyr, saying, "Look what you're doing to us." And if a child does start to tell you about drug use or other forbidden behavior, you can be sure the confidences will end if you break in with "that's disgusting" or some other sign of shock or disapproval. This doesn't mean you have to accept everything your child says and does without criticism. It does mean that you have to wait until the child has finished and then say what you think as calmly and as clearly as you possibly can.

An overeager parent who is committed to "communicating" can also shut off confidences by going too far and too fast. The mother of a teenage daughter who was a favorite with the boys in her school suddenly asked her one Sunday morning, "Do you like being kissed?" When the answer was vague, the mother went on, "How does it feel? Or don't you kiss boys?" With such an onslaught, the daughter understandably disappeared upstairs and didn't come down until lunchtime. With this kind of intrusion, a child will back off and the door between parent and child will be closed. When the subject is drugs, the door may be slammed even more rapidly and closed more tightly.

WHEN TO TALK ABOUT DRUGS AND ALCOHOL

When a child, or anyone, for that matter, is high on drugs or alcohol, it is not the time to try to talk. The child can't hear or understand what you have to say, nor can he or she respond sensibly. By the next day, the child may have forgotten everything you've said. As Deacon Farrell Hopkins, an early leader in drug abuse prevention for the Archdiocese of New York, pointed out, "With the drug in him, that's not your child. Be very careful. He'll fight physically. He'll be abusive verbally. Stay out of it." Later, when the chemicals are out of his body and the anger level has subsided, you can say what you have to say.

One evening a mother smelled marijuana smoke coming from her daughter's bedroom where three girls were having a sleep-over. Her impulse was to rush in, accuse them of smoking, and tell her daughter in no uncertain terms that she would be punished for breaking house rules. Instead, she knocked on the door, calmly asked them to stop, and walked out. The next day she discussed what had happened with her daughter privately and made clear that it mustn't happen again. It didn't. If she had humiliated her daughter in front of her friends, or if she had screamed, "Don't ever bring that stuff into my house," things could have escalated out of control, or the girl might have felt she had to fight back for what she considered her rights.

WHAT TO SAY ABOUT DRUGS AND ALCOHOL

It is helpful to practice what you're going to say the morning after by thinking about it beforehand, and playing both parts, yourself and your child. How can you best get your message across? What will the youngster have to say? What does he or she feel? And what do you want to accomplish, given inescapable societal pressures? This kind of preparation can avoid a shouting match that accomplishes nothing.

What Deacon Hopkins recommended is that you start by telling the child how you really feel underneath the rage and upset. "I love you and I'll do everything I can to help you" is one way to start. "Then," he adds, "you'd better mean it."

If you say, "I'll help you cut loose from some of your fringey friends. I'll play the bad guy and tell them that they can't come in," you must really do it.

"In the late sixties and seventies," Cheryl Rugg, formerly head of the adolescent treatment service at a hospital in Milwaukee, recalls, "there was great emphasis on the kid having a big voice in determining what he did and what the consequences should be. I believe you have to clarify things. You have to say, 'I'm the parent and you're the child and this is what you can expect.'"

MYTHS

Myths have grown out of the sixties experience. One of them is that if you don't talk about it, it will go away. Another is that if you do talk about it, it will be okay. A bewildered mother who believed this, and whose son became seriously involved with cocaine, kept repeating, "But we communicated. We talked a lot. I don't understand how this could have happened."

Another myth is that information about drugs and alcohol will give youngsters all they need to resist the pressure to use illicit substances. Of course, a parent has to give children the facts to counteract the misinformation they pick up from their friends. But research has shown that isn't enough. A parent's example and practical ways of dealing with the everyday world have to be part of the equation. The conversation must include how to say no and how to resist peer pressure.

What is a fifth-grader going to say when someone he's known since kindergarten offers him a puff in the boy's room? What's a fifteen-year-old girl going to say when she believes that her popularity depends on joining a cigarette "break" on the fire escape? How can a father say with conviction, "You don't have to do what everyone's doing," as he regularly pours his predinner drink and chain-smokes? Parents are models for their children. At the very least they must explain that there are behaviors that may be appropriate for adults but are not acceptable for adolescents. And they need to be able to explain why that is so.

Parents also can help their children learn ways to say no to alcohol and drugs comfortably. You might suggest that they say, "No, thanks, I have other things to do today"; "No, thanks, I've got to be with it"; "No, thanks, I usually end up embarrassing myself."

It may all come down to the advice Dr. Mitchell Rosenthal, president of Phoenix House, a pioneering drug treatment facility, gives parents: "It's foolish to scare . . . and essential to prepare." If you warn your child, "Smoke a joint and you will grow up to be an addict," he or she will stop listening. This contradicts his day-to-day experience and that of his friends. Besides, it is an exaggerated statement of what is known about "gateway" or starter drugs and what their use can lead to. Most youngsters never go on to other illicit drugs after they try marijuana. With teenagers, you can focus on a risk you both recognize: "Drinking or smoking pot and driving don't mix. Your reflexes aren't what they should be, you can't judge distance very well, and you can fool yourself into feeling you're driving better than you really are." Deaths on the highway are very much a part of their own experience. As for cigarette smoking, you can focus on the unpleasant reality that smokers' teeth turn yellow, their clothes smell awful, and they develop annoying hacking coughs.

In many ways, though, a youngster sees the world of drug and alcohol use from a perspective that is quite different from that of adults.

What Kids Say:	What Parents Say:
Everybody's doing it.	Not my kid.
I'm not hurting anyone.	This is risky behavior.
I won't snitch on friends.	I expect you to tell me the truth about what is going on.
Every time he opens his mouth he gives me a lecture.	We communicate very well.
If I had too much to drink and called home for a ride, he'd kill me.	I'd kill him.

The last item is the only point of agreement. With such divergent viewpoints, it's no wonder conversations degenerate into battles. One therapist says that often "it's impossible to sit in the same room with the parents and the child without wearing a flak jacket." And yet youngsters have told researchers they want to talk to their parents about drugs and other things that worry them. One boy said, "I kept hoping my parents would ask me what I was doing with my friends. They finally did. I could never bring it up myself."

Sometimes it works out better if you keep in touch with your child at a distance, particularly if the child lives away from home or you are usually at work. Using the phone instead of meeting face-to-face can provide needed distance that could make each of you more comfortable. You will have more control in terms of who initiates the call, and, of course, either person can hang up when there seems to be nothing more to say. Some people find it easier to restrain their emotions on the phone. Body language (facial contortions, a tightened fist, tears) will not be seen and your voice and words alone will have to convey the message. It may feel safer this way. You may want to use the phone when you are very riled up. It certainly should be considered as an alternative way of talking to each other.

DIFFERENT AGES, DIFFERENT STAGES

Conversations with your children have to be appropriate to the child's age and ability to comprehend. Toddlers can be encouraged to tell you what happened at day care or a fourth-grader can discuss what he liked best in his school lunch. Later, attitudes about drinking, smoking, and taking drugs can be passed on by comments while watching television—what the experts call a "teachable moment." A program can prompt a discussion of whether you really need to drink beer to have a good time or make friends. Or you can talk to your children about people they know and what they eat, drink, or smoke. Do so in a way that doesn't denigrate friends or relatives and remains factual and nonjudgmental.

Fifth grade seems to be a particularly good time to talk with children about what is troubling them. At that time they want to talk to you. By sixth grade, they are really worried about alcohol. Concerns probably peak at that age because these kids are on the threshold of junior high school, where they know pressures to drink and use marijuana will increase dramatically. Seventh-grade children (beginning adolescence) start to be more secretive. They don't want anyone to know what goes on. They all try to sit unnoticed in the last row in a classroom.

Even if you've talked to your children through the years, you have to keep repeating the same messages over and over again in different ways. This takes ingenuity. What you say must continue to reflect what they can understand. At times they may not seem to be listening, but they are absorbing your attitudes and ways nevertheless.

It's best to begin this process while your children are very young, since it is hard to communicate about sensitive topics with a defensive teenager who has never developed a feeling of give-and-take with his parents. By the time you say, as one father did, "My son is seventeen. He smokes pot every day. What do I do now?" it may be much harder to start a dialogue. You may need to get outside help to guide you in dealing with the situation.

But even if it is late for him, it is not late to start talking to your younger children. By developing an atmosphere of openness, you might be able to protect the younger ones from repeating the experiences of the older children in the family. This does not mean that you should hold up the older ones as villains or failures, or give up on them. In fact, it will be best to omit comparisons and focus on what goes on in the present.

When a pediatrician asked his ten-year-old son to describe himself, starting with "I'm Bill," the boy wrote: "My father is a doctor. My mother works in the PTA. My sister is a pain." He defined himself in terms of his family with very little awareness of his own qualities. At that age he was still tied to concrete thinking, dealing with what existed in the present rather than with the anticipation of the future. When you talk to a young child you can't say, "If you smoke you'll have lung cancer in forty years." He may believe you, but he simply cannot worry about what might happen in years to come. You have to stick to the immediate and then you will be heard. "If you drink too much, you'll feel awful."

Bill's teenage sister, on the other hand, when asked to describe herself wrote, "I'm pretty. My hair is long and brown. I'm going to be a dancer when I grow up." Perhaps she was something of a pain. But she had a vision of herself as a unique individual, and she was able to project herself into the future. This difference in the ability to abstract may reflect real structural differences in the brain, and that slow maturational process must be taken into account as you communicate with your children.

GETTING AT THE TRUTH

Often parents really don't want to hear about their children's experiences smoking marijuana or popping pills. They ask tentative questions ("You're not smoking, are you?"), don't wait for the answer, and then quickly drop the subject. Many children are consummate con artists. They tell parents what they want to hear. This combination of denial on both the parent's and the child's part, plus untruthfulness, keeps the whole subject under cover.

Here are some suggestions for getting beyond the barrier:

- Learn from your child. Ask for information: "Could you tell me more about that?" "What is that?" Keep the conversation going.

- Don't ask, "Why did you do it?" In all probability your child doesn't know and you'll simply be putting him in an impossible spot. Many of us don't know why we do some of the things we do.

A parent has to avoid putting the teenager on the defensive, and that isn't easy. Many counselors who work with youngsters have learned to avoid certain approaches that tend to lead nowhere. They do not:

- Accuse ("You're lying and you know it!").
- Label ("You're a pothead").
- Belittle friends ("They're a bunch of losers").

Instead, they become allies, by listening or by saying, in effect, "I understand that you want to do what your friends do. I'm concerned. What can we do?"

If you suspect that your child is using drugs, what is there to say? Some parents have begun by talking about themselves and their own daredevil behavior or their own experimentation when they were growing up. This diminishes the "us against them" attitude that pits parents against teenagers. Other parents begin by referring to an article in the paper about an accident caused by drinking and driving or a DWI arrest. Or they may come up with something on the drinking age or school and community policy or legal issues. Others come right out with it by talking about themselves and how upset they feel now that they know that their child is drinking too much or using illicit drugs.

Some parents prepare to deal with their own children by recalling how they were treated by their parents and what their feelings were on the subject of drugs and drinking. First you can consider how they spoke to you, what they expected of you, how much they trusted you, and the degree to which you were consulted when it came to family decision-making. You may also be able to remember how you felt about your parents when they were setting limits or treating you in ways that you felt were unfair and frightening.

They may have set curfews earlier than those of your friends. They may have threatened you with harsh punishments. Sometimes they followed through on those threats. A woman remembers the time her father pulled his belt out of its loops and hit her across the back. From that day on she lived in fear of his power and bursts of anger.

If your parents were (or are) heavy drug users or drinkers, there are some special concerns that you must have. Their erratic behavior did not provide a model of good parenting. There were probably unshared family secrets. You will need to learn how to share them with your own children and keep the lines open between family members. And there was probably a lot of fighting, which is not a helpful approach when you are trying to deal effectively and rationally with your own children's drug and alcohol use.

If your parents didn't talk to you but only gave directions—"Pick up your clothing"; "Empty the garbage"; "Stop picking your pimples"—you know that those commands did not lead to interchanges but brought conversation to a grinding halt. You may have had very little practice in family dialogue.

Even when a child does talk about what goes on, there are certain peer rules that may differ from those of the child's parents. You may expect the truth, but a child may face ostracism if he or she "tells" on a friend. So what seems like a simple question about the party Friday night may really raise complex ethical or moral conflicts. The child may have to ask himself, "Do I squeal on my friends? Do I change the subject and cover it up? Do I misrepresent the truth? If I talk about what I did, not what others did, will my parents understand?"

Young people are often left in limbo, particularly if they feel they can't count on their parents. One of the goals you will achieve by keeping the lines of communication open is a sense of trust between family members that will go a long way toward helping your children make decisions for themselves that will make sense to you. Whatever comes out in a conversation, a child has to know that talking isn't the end of loving, or of hoping that things can be better.

5

Parent Power

Parental authority is a fact of life. It can be used very lovingly. I have seen terrible situations turn around when parents have said "enough is enough." Vulnerable youngsters cannot save themselves. This is where parents come in.

—DR. HAROLD VOTH, UNIVERSITY OF KANSAS MEDICAL CENTER

It's Sunday night, you've finished raking leaves, and you're watching TV. You have that awful feeling of being totally alone, although you can hear neighbors slam doors and one of your children is begging for a snack. You feel alone facing the problem of what to do about your youngster who, during seventh grade, has changed from a sweet compliant child into a "monster." You know, intellectually, that young adolescents do this, but you suspect it is more than that. More than once, you have found cigarette butts in the bushes or smelled the acrid smoke of marijuana in her clothing after she has left friends just outside the front door.

But you are not alone and you are not helpless. Thousands of other parents are going through the same thing and are doing something about it. Here are ten tips for parents who, like you, are concerned about their teenagers' exposure to tobacco, drugs, and alcohol:

TIPS FOR PARENTS

1. To minimize conflict, have clear rules and clear consequences if rules are disobeyed. Teenagers are naturally rebellious and want to see how far they can go; but many of them say they "want parents to be bastards" so they can get out of doing what they really don't want to do with their friends. Remind yourself and them that a family is not a democracy.

2. If your rules are ignored, invoke the consequences that have been stated. Do this every time a rule is broken, without exception. You can cut allowances or reduce telephone or driving privileges. Grounding is often the most effective punishment—but remember, you will have to stay in, too. Unfortunately, sanctions such as these may be futile if your child is already heavily involved in drug use. They are most likely to work if the problem hasn't gotten out of hand.

3. If you want to make your rules stick, join with the parents of your kid's friends, at least by telephone, to check on the realities of overnights, parties, and curfews. Monitor your child's activities, and express unmistakable disapproval of problem behavior.

4. If you want to protect your children, give them very

clear messages about how you feel about alcohol, tobacco, drugs, sex, etc. If the child has no idea what you
believe or receives mixed messages, he or she will be
confused and therefore vulnerable.

5. If you want your children to respect what you say, learn
more than they know. With accurate information you
can combat misinformation and inform your other
children. You can help them evaluate critically what
they hear from friends, see on television or on the Internet, and read in the pamphlets they bring home
from school.

6. If your child is closely tied to a peer group, remember
that you still have influence. Teenagers need parents
and other adults as models and guides through the
minefields of moral development.

7. If your child is running with an inappropriate group,
try to identify and encourage his other, non-using
friends. Include them in family outings and invite
them over to eat. Most kids have links to more than
one group. If you are desperate, cut the destructive al-
legiance. Your child will protest but may ultimately be
relieved. One expert suggests you change schools or
move, if that's the only way. Sometimes you can switch
school districts in your own town or pay a small sum
for your child to attend school in a neighboring community. If you want your child to give up his old
group, you may have to take up the slack by spending
more time with him, doing things he enjoys, working
on ways to make your relationship better.

8. If your child says, "Of course not—don't you trust
me?" when challenged about drug use, explain that

you can't surrender your role as a parent. You are concerned and responsible.

9. If your child is using, talk about it with someone you trust. Fear of ridicule, criticism, or gossip may be keeping you quiet and immobilizing you. If you discuss your problems, you may find to your amazement that your friend or coworker has a similar story and can help you take action.

10. If your child doesn't see a need to change or won't get help, get it for yourself. You may not be able to change your child, but you can change yourself and feel less overwhelmed.

Underlying these suggestions are two realities: You can't control your child's behavior, and parents have rights. You shouldn't have to worry that your child (or his friend) is going to steal from you or that your child is going to hurt you. You have the right to say, "Either follow the rules, get into treatment, or get out."

Somewhere along the line, parents have lost confidence in their own judgment. They think they don't know enough or don't understand enough, and they turn to the experts. (That's why you're reading this book.) But common sense based on life experience is still a good guide when coupled with accurate information. Trust yourself. Youngsters often perceive adults as having much more power than the grown-ups themselves would believe. The following list of hard-hitting guidelines was prepared by boys spending time in a correctional facility in North Carolina. The youngsters clearly had adult help in putting this together, but there is enough authenticity left to help you see yourself as your children may see you.

1. Keep cool. Don't lose your temper in the crunch. Keep the lid on when things go wrong. Children are great imitators.
2. Bug us a little. Be strict and consistent in dishing out discipline. It gives us a feeling of security to know we've got some strong support under us.
3. Don't blow your class. Keep the dignity of parenthood. Stay on that pedestal. Do not try to dress, dance, or talk like your kids. You embarrass us and you look ridiculous.
4. Scare the hell out of us. If you catch us lying, stealing, or being cruel, get tough. Let us know why what we did was wrong. Impress on us the importance of not repeating such behavior. But let us know you still love us, even though we have let you down.
5. Call our bluff. Make it clear that you mean what you say. And don't be intimidated by our threats to drop out of school or leave home. Stand firm. If you collapse, we will know we beat you down and we will not be happy with the "victory." Kids don't want everything they ask for.

What do kids need from their parents in order to find their way safely to adulthood? According to the experts and adolescents themselves, they need:

• Trust and support. (A study of seven thousand youngsters showed that those who didn't have the trust and support of their parents were more likely to cave in to peer pressure.)
• Realistically high academic standards.
• The chance to succeed.
• The chance to fail and still be accepted.

- Praise, love, and physical touching. (The "Did you hug your kid today?" bumper stickers apply to kids as tall as you are as well as to toddlers. The adolescents sometimes cringe, but don't let that inhibit you.)

PARENTS HELPING PARENTS

It is a lot easier to follow suggestions such as these if you stand together with other parents. A mother from Delaware says, "I believe strongly in parents getting together for education and support. It's the only way I have survived parenthood—that and Erma Bombeck."

Across the country, many parent groups provide information, emotional support, and community action aimed at stemming the flood of alcohol and drug abuse among young people. If peer pressure works to push teenagers into drug use, parental peer pressure can also provide a united front against such activities. No matter how clear you are about rules and regulations, you will have a hard time enforcing them alone. Parent peer groups help you see that you are not alone and provide concrete suggestions for dealing with common problems. Meetings are often announced in local newspapers, and some are sponsored by schools and churches.

GETTING A PARENT GROUP STARTED

If there is no parent group in your area, you can start one with the help of other concerned parents. One community began a group that now meets regularly in a youth center by placing an ad in the local paper. It read: "ATTENTION, PARENTS! Share your concerns with other parents of preteens and teens. Join a parent-support group. For more information call . . ."

A group in Berkeley, California, was organized initially to raise awareness about drugs, but it then went on to other things. The group got the neighborhood high school to inform parents immediately when children cut class and raised enough money for a full-page ad in their local newspaper. This one said, "We think Berkeley youth have a drug problem," and was signed by school administrators, judges, and others who deal with kids. "Once they signed," says a founding mother, "they couldn't back down later and say there's no problem." National organizations such as PRIDE (National Parents' Resource Institute for Drug Education) can help you organize and provide you with educational materials. (See page 231 for information.) These support groups are not "therapy groups." Nor are they necessarily for parents whose children are in deep trouble. By joining one, you're not saying you are sick, bad, or weak, or have a "freaky" child. You are saying only that you are concerned, and intelligent enough to do something about it.

Groups vary a great deal. Some have professional leadership; others are basically self-help with no leader or rotating leaders. What is it like to join one? One mother whose son's drug use was disrupting the lives of everyone close to him finally made the decision to go alone to her local group. "As I drove up to the house," she recalls, "I kept hoping I'd come to the wrong address and this would turn out to be a Tupperware party." Once she was welcomed, she found she had a lot in common with the other members. They, too, had children who were involved with drugs or alcohol. They, too, were in great distress, feeling anxious, guilty, and frustrated.

In one group a father said he would never understand why he got so angry with his fourteen-year-old daughter that he hit her on the arm and gave her a huge black-and-blue mark. He was near tears. Another group member immediately reassured him, saying he had done exactly the same thing to his own twelve-year-old daughter, then added, "There are times when it is just about impossible to control your anger, particularly after a child has been warned many times that coming in after nine o'clock on week nights is unacceptable."

Such fathers are unusual. Support groups are generally made up of mothers only—not surprising when we look at who goes for help in our society. In a support group, whether made up of fathers, mothers, or a combination, you will get some practical answers to questions such as "What do I say when my kid uses foul language?" ("That's easy," said one mother. "He's off the basketball team.") "What can I do? I'm in a real bind. My kid delivers newspapers. He owes the company seventy dollars. He collected the money from customers and used it for God knows what. If I don't fork over the money, he's going to be in real trouble." ("He is in real trouble," another mother said. "Let him see what the real world is about—he sells his drums, quick.")

Support groups not only provide information, understanding, and practical advice, but they also give parents an opportunity to know the parents of their child's friends and exchange phone numbers. Then they can make rules and policies together to strengthen the network and take action.

TOUGHLOVE

If your child is already using drugs or alcohol destructively, you might want to consider a support group designed specifically for parents with troubled, drug-using children. Toughlove, based in Doylestown, Pennsylvania, is one of the most widely known parent support groups. More than one thousand such groups are at work worldwide. Toughlove is based on an action program with clear-cut consequences for unacceptable behavior. You will find ardent supporters of this approach, and also harsh critics. The only way to tell if it is for you is to read Toughlove literature and attend some meetings. For information, look in your local library or call Toughlove, listed in your phone book. "We were ready for any help we could get, because we were watching our son totally deteriorate," says one father. Because he had run through all his money, his son, heavily involved in cocaine, asked if he could come back home after living in his own place for several months. His parents, who felt sorry for him, brought his request to the group meeting. The group "offered us support and encouragement along with their opinion that we had been too soft when faced with unacceptable behavior." With this backing, the parents were able to say firmly that he could not live at home as long as he kept using drugs. He stayed with friends, then got a job and an apartment. During the summer, he studied and got his high school diploma (he'd dropped out the year before). Now he is living at home and attending college. His mother says, "We feel that the emotional support and helpful suggestions of the Toughlove group were instrumental in changing our behavior, and this seemed to help our son become much more responsible instead of mouthing empty promises."

Sometimes parents have acted abruptly and then come to Toughlove for support. One middle-aged father said at his first meeting, "Our kid came in drunk last night. We'd had it, both of us. We told him to get out of the house and take his junk with him." Instead of giving them approval for this ultimate act, the people in the group suggested that there were steps they could have taken before they barred the boy from the house, such as spelling out more definitively the consequences of drinking too much or waiting until the next day when the sober youth would be more able to understand their actions. Then, if he should continue to drink, in spite of their warnings, they could resort to locking him out. The objective is to provide the youngster with options, and if he does not choose any of them, the penalties are nonnegotiable.

FAMILIES ANONYMOUS

Families Anonymous, based in Culver City, California, is another group that helps parents feel more powerful and take a firm stand. Although parents cannot keep their child from using drugs, they can learn to avoid standing in the way of their child's recovery from the illness. They can be helped to let the child take more responsibility for what happens to him or her, yet realistically, parents cannot walk away from their child's problems. That's why some parents find Families Anonymous more compatible than the traditional distancing attitude of Al-Anon (discussed below). A parent who had been going to Al-Anon switched to Families Anonymous because "we kept hearing about taking care of ourselves and forgetting about the person who was using drugs. But we're dealing with children, not spouses, and we have a different quality of responsibility for them."

One father started a meeting by saying, "I'm frantic and I shouldn't be. It's my son who's in debt and still borrowing to buy pot. Why am I the scared one? He's got the problem, but I can't seem to help, although I've tried everything." Another harassed father joined in: "I bailed my kid out for the fourth time last night. He drove the car into a ditch and we had to get the tow truck. I don't want the kid in the clinker, but maybe it would serve him right." Both fathers were helped to see that they had to let their children feel the results of their actions—no matter how painful it might be for both parents and child. And they had to stand by with the offer of support and counseling when the appropriate time came.

If a Families Anonymous group is not convenient to you, you're sure to find an Al-Anon group. Al-Anon helps those who are married to an alcoholic, or have family members or friends whose drinking is affecting their lives. Now it has many members who are parents concerned about their children. It may or may not be the right place for you. Some parents find the spiritual aspects of Al-Anon, which is based on the twelve steps of Alcoholics Anonymous, a great comfort when they feel cornered. Others are troubled by what seem to them approaches that work with adults but are less applicable to children. Equally helpful, although not as widespread, are Nar-Anon groups for families and friends of drug abusers. Their meetings, too, are based on the twelve steps of AA. Information on Nar-Anon can be obtained by calling any local Narcotics Anonymous (NA) listing. If you find Al-Anon or Nar-Anon is not what you're looking for, you may want to start a Families Anonymous group. (See page 230 for information.)

FAMILY CONTRACTS

Family rules and obligations are sometimes easier to enforce and abide by if you create a family contract. Your children must accept the fact that as long as they live at home, you are responsible for them. Maybe you will feel that a written document is too alien to the way you usually handle things. In that case, you can choose a part of one or use one or two items as discussion points. Even if your children think signing a contract is silly, or something neither they nor their friends would ever do, you can use the idea of spelling things out as a way of talking about concerns you might have been hesitant to approach.

Identifying areas that have led to family discord and straightening out such matters as curfews, mealtimes, and chore assignments can minimize the conflict. Hammering out a contract, whether or not the family is in some sort of group therapy, can teach your children that a dispute can be handled by all members speaking out, exploring the problem jointly, and finally coming to a compromise. If a parent imposes his ideas on everyone else without a discussion, children are left dissatisfied and angry. "I'm the boss here," said one father. "I earn the money—this is my home—and what I say goes! Don't you forget it!" This kind of rigidity will almost surely turn kids off and invite rebellion. Here is a sample for you to use as a framework for devising your own contract. Keep in mind that even young children can assume responsibilities. A family may not be a democracy, but neither is it a dictatorship, and dialogue is essential. Let everyone help create this document so it will have meaning for all, like a family construction project.

SAMPLE FAMILY CONTRACT

Dates during which contract is to be in force:
Parents and children will:

1. Not physically or verbally abuse one another,
2. Be as honest as possible with each other.
3. Not judge one another harshly.
4. Arrange a family discussion or ask that one be arranged so that any part of this contract can be changed.

Children will:

1. Help with the household chores. (Chores are to be enumerated here. They will depend on living arrangements, age of the child, and number of siblings living at home and will include such items as laundry, garbage, pet care, lawn care, dishwashing, preparations for school or work, etc.)
2. Not use any drug (not prescribed by a physician) or smoke or drink any alcoholic beverage if they are below the legal age.
3. Observe agreed-upon curfews. (Curfews should be set in accordance with the age of the child.)
4. Attend therapy sessions if these have been agreed upon.

Parents will:

1. Attend family therapy sessions if these are part of a treatment plan.
2. Monitor their own use of tobacco, alcohol, caffeine, or other mood-altering substances.

Consequences of breaking contract:

1. One trespass will lead to a family conference.
2. Two trespasses will lead to the family meeting with a counselor to determine specific consequences. (Remember that grounding an angry teenager can be harder on the people with whom he lives than on the person confined to the house.)

When parents recognize their own trespasses, they certainly should bring them up for discussion. Again, keep in mind that you as a parent are a person with certain standards and needs. Your child has to learn, albeit at his or her own pace, that you are not perfect, you are vulnerable, and you, too, have feelings that may be expressed.

If formality is your style, when the contract has been agreed upon, it can be signed by all concerned.

AFTER A PARTY, WHAT?

Let's say your child ignores the rules and comes home drunk or stoned. What should you do? First you should:

- Try to remain calm.
- Try to find out what substance he or she has been using. If he or she is incoherent, can't "come down," or becomes unconscious, call 911, call a doctor, or go to an emergency room.
- Check on him or her during the night.
- Wait until the next day to have a conversation.

The next day:

- Have a talk. Try to find out the circumstances under which drugs or alcohol were used.
- Let your son or daughter know you do not condone the use of drugs. If you've said it before, say it again.
- Work out ways your child may be able to avoid situations that lead to continuing drug use.
- Enforce the family rules and do what you said you would do if something like this occurred.

OTHER SUPPORTS

At times, your own power can be increased by turning to a friend, rather than a group. A mother who was herself a recovering alcoholic was concerned about her fourteen-year-old daughter, who had come into the house drunk on several occasions. She tried to get her to accompany her to an AA meeting, but the girl flatly refused, saying, "Stick to your own problems, Mom." This mother then asked one of her AA friends if she would invite the daughter to a meeting in a neighboring town as a way of sidestepping mother-daughter conflict. She explained that the girl was sneaking pre-party drinks from her father's liquor cabinet and drinking anytime she had to face a difficult social situation. Three years later, the young woman thanked her mother for engineering that visit to her first crucial AA meeting.

SCHOOLS

When parents feel overwhelmed by what is going on at home, many of them shift responsibility and blame the school for their children's trouble. You can't expect the school to do your job as a parent, but you can recognize the important role schools play, and work closely with them.

If you are worried about your child, keep in touch with school guidance counselors or psychologists to let them know what is happening at home. Support school discipline, unless you are convinced it is unjust (see page 130). Sometimes well-meaning teachers see class-cutting or a failed test as an isolated incident and never check with a child's other teachers to find out if a problem is serious and pervasive. The guidance office can bring parents, teachers, and students together. Then, too, if your child has been in treatment and is returning to school, the guidance staff can serve as an invaluable liaison with whatever program your child has been in. It is important to keep the lines of communication open so that any warning signs are spotted quickly.

Joining with other parents can help bring about school-related prevention programs, special programs for recovering students, drug education programs, and drug counseling. One parent group raised the money to pay for a drug counselor in the local high school when the school budget had no funds for such a service. Many schools now have student assistance programs, often staffed by counselors from an outside agency to augment and complement the work of busy guidance departments. These counselors are trained to identify and help students whose drug and alcohol use is hurting their school performance, and to work with those who are living with a parental drinking problem. Student assistance programs can reduce the incidence of drug and alcohol use and improve students' attendance at school—results that can lower school dropout rates and teenage pregnancies. The longer a girl stays in school, the less likely she is to become pregnant. These programs guarantee confidentiality, and although your child may not yet be a participant, you can help by supporting the school's efforts. Many parents whose kids are still in trouble become active volunteers in antidrug efforts. At least they feel that they are in control of something, and that their efforts are not entirely futile. They may be able to help someone else's child even if they can't save their own.

Schools are not meant to be treatment centers, nor teachers policemen, but they should carry some responsibility. One Virginia high school student said what cut down on drug use in his school was computerized attendance monitoring. "Just by keeping track of students," he said, "they cut down on our free time to get high." Schools should let parents know when their children are absent or chronically cutting classes, and all personnel should be sophisticated enough to recognize drug-dealing and drug use so that the authorities can act. School smoking rules should be well defined and publicized for parents and teachers as well as students.

Right under the eyes of teachers, the school custodian of a high school in Texas was selling drugs to seniors. And those seniors were selling to juniors. In another school, the major pusher was a school bus driver who hung around the school grounds before the buses left in the afternoons. The dealing was going on as school authorities, untrained to detect these transactions, remained unaware.

Infiltration in this particular school was stopped by an alert parent who overheard his daughter saying to a friend, "Now that school is out I don't know where to get it." This fifteen-year-old was on summer vacation; the school grounds had been her source of pot. Many of her friends had gone away for the summer and she had lost track of her "supplier." Her father mobilized the energy of his parent support group. Several parents talked to the school guidance department. The next year an all-day session was devoted to drug education for all school personnel.

By federal law, drugs are prohibited in the area in and around schools. But, as Joseph Califano, former secretary of health, education and welfare, points out, "A drug-free school in America is an oxymoron. We have to do something about that. We have to do it locally where the parents are, in the family, in the community."

Most schools welcome input from parents, particularly if it is constructive and not confrontational. You can work through organizations such as the Parent-Teacher Association. You can also work with the school board to make sure that your area has a strong, clearly articulated policy about tobacco, alcohol, and other drugs, written with community help, with in-school penalties well publicized and evenhandedly administered. When one school set up such a policy, the first child to break the rules was the mayor's daughter. The penalty fell on her as if she had been any ordinary student—and that gave the program credibility. Some schools now test students for marijuana and other drug use.

You can see to it that people who are appointed or elected to the school board are tuned in to drug questions and are willing to spend money on drug education. (Although no firm evidence exists to prove that current drug education classes work, new approaches seem to offer more hope. They concentrate on showing youngsters specifically how to identify and counter the pressures to use drugs instead of focusing on more abstract facts about drug use.) You can also push for elementary school counselors to intervene with problem kids early enough to short-circuit later drug use. Just your presence at a meeting demonstrates your concern.

THE POLICE

One practical way parents can feel less helpless is to work with the police. They know where and when accidents are likely to occur on Friday and Saturday nights when youngsters drink or use drugs, then drive. Parents can insist that these particular places have heavier police surveillance in order to slow down the hurtling cars or to pick up intoxicated drivers. You can alert the police by a phone call the day before a gathering and tell them where it will be, when it will end, and where the kids might go afterward.

Police and parents cooperating can also defuse the dangerous potential for violence when kids get together in public to drink or use drugs. You shouldn't intervene on your own, but you can notify the police if you see a crowd gathering, and you can demand that they enforce local ordinances about kids congregating.

PARENT POWER IS WORKING

Horrifying numbers of young people abuse alcohol and other drugs, kill themselves and other youngsters on the highways, and recklessly ruin their own lives. But public outrage is having its effect. MADD (Mothers Against Drunk Driving) became a successful national movement after Candy Lightner's daughter was killed by a drinking driver in 1980. The outraged mother established a powerful organization in which parents joined other parents to ensure the safety of their children. Then SADD (Students Against Driving Drunk) was founded by Robert Anastas, a Massachusetts high school teacher. SADD's goal is to make it less socially acceptable for students to drink and drive or accept a ride with anyone who has been drinking. (Some parents feel the SADD contract, which requires a child to call home for a ride if he or she has been drinking, is a subtle way of giving the child permission to drink. The only proper message, say these parents, is "Don't drink at all if you are underage.")

Kids are also banding together to combat the drug culture. Older students are going into the elementary schools to talk to youngsters about the dangers of drugs, and prepare them for the pressures they might meet later. The cumulative efforts of these national and local movements— parents with parents, parents with young people, and kids with kids—are beginning to make a difference.

6

The Law: Knowing It and Using It

It's hard to believe, but the most helpful people were the cops.

—THE MOTHER OF A DRUG-ABUSING SON

The first time you realize there is trouble may be when a policeman turns up on your doorstep with your child in tow or when you get a call from the police station. Try not to panic. Today's police departments and court systems have a wide range of resources designed to help parents and, at the same time, rehabilitate and not necessarily punish youngsters. Juvenile aid bureaus and specially trained po-

Many of the specifies in this chapter are based on the laws of New York State. Laws and regulations vary from state to state and community to community. For legal advice, consult a lawyer.

lice and probation officers are available in many communities to work with young people. As a parent you have to make sure that what really happens fits what is promised and that your child gets the best the system has to offer. Knowing something about the law as it applies to parents and their children can help you deal with the difficulties that may come up if your child is trapped by alcohol or drug abuse.

WHEN YOUR CHILD IS ARRESTED

Youngsters are picked up by the police for all sorts of reasons, major and minor, from knocking over mailboxes to possession of drugs to driving under the influence of alcohol. In every state the use of drugs by a minor (someone under the legal age as far as criminal law is concerned) is classified as juvenile delinquency. In 1994, the National Center for Juvenile Justice reported that approximately one in every sixteen youngsters under the age of eighteen was arrested.

If that call comes from the station house, what should you do? A lawyer with years of experience working with youngsters and their parents says emphatically, "I don't care if it's the middle of the night. You get down there." While in custody, your child (whether he is a juvenile or young adult) has all the federal rights of any arrested person. These include:

- The right to remain silent.
- The right to answer some questions and not others. For example, the child might answer the question "Were you

on Main Street at nine o'clock this evening?" and later refuse to answer the question "Was Johnny Jones with you?" Answering basic questions such as "What is your name?" and "What is your address?" in a cooperative way may satisfy the police, forestall a formal arrest, and avoid more serious consequences.

- The right to call parents or a lawyer.
- The right to have a lawyer present during questioning.
- The right to refuse to consent to anything, sign anything, or offer any information. (However, if the charge is a minor one, signing a waiver of some of these basic rights—to have a lawyer present, for example—can sometimes result in more lenient treatment, because it makes things simpler for the police. If the charge is serious, a waiver should not be signed.)

If your child is still a minor (the age at which one is legally an adult varies from sixteen to twenty-one, depending on the state), the police are required to call and tell you where he or she is, and to have you present when the child is questioned. If you are not in the room, whatever your child says is off the record and can't be used in any later proceeding.

How your child's case will be handled depends on what he or she has done, what alternatives are available in your community, and whether your child has been in trouble with the law before. Here are some possibilities:

- Your child may be sent home with a warning. A petty first offense is often handled informally. Says a detective in upstate New York: "If a kid comes from a solid family just a few blocks away, we're not going to hold him or charge him. Sometimes we drive him home. Sometimes we call the parents."

- Your child may be diverted from the juvenile justice system. Some communities have youth courts run by youngsters themselves to hear petty cases and mete out punishment. Direct referral to a mental health agency for treatment is another possibility. In New York State, youngsters who are unmanageable, truants, or runaways (known as status offenders in legal terms) can be handled this way. The clout of the law stands behind the referral, since the youths can be brought to court if they do not cooperate.

- Your child may be referred to the probation department. (In place of a jail term for a young adult or detention in a juvenile facility for a child, probation provides supervision.) Sometimes there is a formal court hearing before a youngster is placed on probation; other times the case never gets to court. Although every locality has its own laws and methods, the first step is usually a conference of parents, child, and probation officer to assess the situation and plan procedures. The child may have to do weekly public service; he or she will probably have to come in and talk to the probation officer every week; and the officer may require tests for substance abuse and, if they are positive, an evaluation to determine how bad things are. Counseling, too, can be required. Sometimes this "social work" under the umbrella of the law is all that is needed. If it doesn't work and the child does not comply with the requirements, the case can be brought before a judge.

- Your child may be brought to court for a hearing. Since juvenile court proceedings were designed to provide help rather than punishment, they do not usually have the trappings of a trial. Instead, a child appears before a judge who determines what the next step will be. However, if your child stands the chance of being sent away to a juvenile detention facility, he or she is entitled to most of the rights of an adult, including the right to have a lawyer present, to cross-examine witnesses, and to provide defense witnesses. Even if your child (as a juvenile) is convicted, there will be no public record.

- Your child may be issued a citation. Some states—Florida, Minnesota, North Carolina, and Idaho among them—recently made it illegal for those underage to possess tobacco and tobacco products. Youngsters caught smoking may be required to pay a fine, do community service, or appear in court with a parent for an educational program. Repeat offenders may face loss of drivers' licenses or even, in Idaho, time in a juvenile detention facility. Smoking is an "infraction," not a criminal offense, and will not be on your child's record.

SHOULD YOU HIRE A LAWYER?

Under most circumstances you probably do not need to hire a lawyer. But if the offense is serious and you want to contest the allegations or get your child off, you will need one promptly. The lawyer's first suggestion will probably be, "Don't answer any questions." He or she can help you and your child keep from making damaging statements and perhaps arrange for your child's release.

If you cannot afford a lawyer and your child is legally an adult, the court will appoint one if the case is scheduled to go to court. For juveniles who will appear before a judge, a lawyer is automatically appointed regardless of family finances. Despite this protection, you may still want to consider hiring your own private lawyer. Court-appointed lawyers don't come into the picture immediately, and if there is a real question of guilt or innocence or if the offense is a grave one, you may want an attorney there from the very start.

In addition to guarding your child's rights, lawyers can be helpful in other ways. Take the case of Mary.

One Saturday night she and a girlfriend went pub-hopping from shopping center to shopping center with two boys, one of them old enough to buy alcohol. Mary was driving, and after the last drinking stop she was taking the boys home when she hit a fence. She drove on, dropped the boys off, then sideswiped a car. The driver of the car called the police, who found Mary and her friend (who was bleeding from a cut on the forehead) a few blocks away with the car half in a ditch. Mary's blood alcohol level was .20—double the usual legal limit. She was charged with driving while intoxicated and leaving the scene of two accidents. These offenses were so serious that the judge had the option of treating her as an adult although she was only seventeen and legally a juvenile in her state.

The next morning her father called his lawyer and went with Mary to the lawyer's office for a conference.

The lawyer asked her some probing questions:

"How often do you drink?" ("Just with my friends.")

"How often is that?" ("Three or four times a week.")

"Do you ever drink alone?" ("Yes.")

"So you drink every day." ("Yes.")

And the final shocker: "Have you ever considered the possibility that you are an alcoholic?"

No one had thought about that. But Mary said she had no memory of driving the boys home or the accidents. With this admission, Mary's father acknowledged that he, too, had gone through a period in his life when he had a drinking problem.

Even before the case came to court, the lawyer helped Mary's family to establish a curfew for her, take away the car keys because she was a danger to herself and others, and end her relationships with her "friends."

Mary then went away to a ninety-day treatment program for alcoholism and other drug abuse. There she attended courses and got enough credits to graduate with her class.

At the court hearing, Mary's lawyer told the judge that she was in treatment and pointed out that this was the best way to keep Mary from hurting anyone, including herself. He also said that Mary had agreed to work and pay half his fee. Impressed by the progress Mary had already made, the judge held off on his decision for four months and said that if everything went well, he would dismiss the case. The lawyer's fee arrangement, incidentally, is one that is recommended if a child tangles with the law. If damages are required, the child should also pay at least part. Otherwise, a parent colludes in allowing the child to evade responsibilities.

As Mary's story illustrates, a lawyer can assist the family in laying down firm rules and sticking to them, navigate the justice system to get the best help for the child, and enable the family to understand what is happening and why.

The decision to hire a lawyer depends not only on the

services he or she can render, but on your ability to pay and on how involved you want to be, particularly if your child is older and has a history of trouble with the law.

USING THE LAW TO HELP

Sometimes the force of law is necessary to get a child to accept help. A parent's asking the court to step in and order treatment is called "creative coercion" by Peter B. Rockholz, a Connecticut social worker with more than a decade of experience in the residential treatment of young alcohol and drug abusers. "It's important to involve the law as an ally while your child is still a juvenile," he says. "Often we wait too long. Some kids have to be taken away from their home and friends in order to get better, and a judge can arrange this most readily before the kid has to be treated as an adult." If the court's order is disobeyed, the youngster can be sent to a juvenile detention facility. The message is: "Get treatment or be treated as a delinquent."

When a problem reaches crisis proportions, the court can step in quickly. One family brought their fourteen-year-old son to the probation department when his alcohol and drug use and fighting at home had become unbearable. The boy was so out of control the judge swiftly sent him to the local youth shelter for the night, and the next day he was in a thirty-day treatment center. "Some places say the kids must be motivated before they take them," the probation officer on the case says, "but that's nonsense. Most kids have to be pushed, and when they need help they need it now. The judge did the pushing."

The law can also be helpful in insisting that a child take

treatment seriously. Mr. Rockholz worked with a boy who had been warned three times before coming into his facility, "Either give us your drugs or flush them down the toilet yourself, but no drugs are allowed here." When the boy arrived for his stay, he had two marijuana joints hidden in his socks, although he swore he was clean. "We called the cops and they arrested him," he reports. "It had a profound impact on treatment. He knew we meant what we said, and he stuck with us."

Even when a child is older and living on his own, the authority of the law can move him into treatment. Here's how one parent succeeded.

A father had been getting enormous bills from the local furniture store because his son had been charging items and selling them to support his drug habit. Realizing that it is not always best to rescue your child, this man called the store and told the manager not to sell any more goods to his son. If he came in and attempted to charge anything, the manager should call the police.

One day the father received a call from the store manager, who said his son was there buying a sofa bed. The father simply said, "Call the police." Then he went downtown and stood in the aisle as the police arrested his son and took him to be booked for unlawful use of a credit card. This event shook the young man so severely that it turned the tide. The court ordered him into treatment. Now, two years later, he's living drug-free and is buying his household needs and everything else with cash.

Some parents threaten to bring their children to court as they used to threaten them with the bogeyman or the policeman. If you say, "I'm going to take you to court if you don't straighten out," be prepared for some uncomfortable times. Unless there is a crisis necessitating immediate action, the first appearance before a judge or with a probation officer is never satisfying, according to a Washington, D.C., counselor who works closely with the juvenile courts. In addition, the procedure after that first day in court or the probation office is likely to take months. Your child's reaction may be to think, "It's not such a big deal." If you do make the move, you have to be prepared to follow through with constructive action during the lull. One boy had to stay home while his school soccer team went to play in Ireland. His parents were determined that life would not just drift along as usual. When he made his second appearance at the probation department, he was ready to follow the officer's recommendation to see a counselor.

THE LAW AND THE SCHOOLS

Since schools are where the kids are—or should be—most of the time, they are often the setting for the discovery of the drug problem or for conflicts because of it. Parents sometimes saddle them with both the blame and the responsibility. Yet, as an administrator points out, although "the parents think the schools should crack down on drugs and the schools and cops think it is the parents' job, the truth is, none of us can do it alone." Essentially, the schools are responsible for what happens in school and on their grounds and the police are called in only as a last resort or if a crime has been committed. Once in a while, they go into the schools as undercover agents to expose extensive drug-dealing, but in general, they stay away. Parents, on the other hand, are intimately involved with the school's impact on their children's lives.

To be able to act effectively, parents should be aware of the legal background behind what the school may and may not do. Local and state regulations differ, but there are some federal rules that apply to all schools:

- It is a federal crime to sell drugs in or near a public or private school.
- Schools can make unannounced searches of lockers, rest rooms, and "smoking areas," particularly if school policy on these matters was written and distributed at the start of the school year.
- Schools may, under certain circumstances, search students and their lockers with less stringent requirements than the police are required to use, but must still follow "reasonable guidelines." The legality of the search may depend on the reason for it and how intrusive it is.
- Student athletes may be required to submit to random drug testing.
- Schools may expel or discipline a student without waiting for the outcome of court proceedings.
- If the school wants to suspend a child for a short time because of behavior related to drug or alcohol use, the child and his parents have the right to know the charges and what evidence the school has, and to present their side of the story and question witnesses at an informal conference.
- If the suspension is for a longer time, a formal hearing must be held, with an impartial person hearing the charges and the opportunity for cross-examination of

witnesses. (In some states, if your child is suspended for more than ten days and is too young to be finished with school legally, an alternative education must be provided.)

Private schools, too, must follow these rules. In some, the policy is that a child caught with drugs or alcohol should have a second chance and should not be expelled. But as one headmaster put it, "We think he should have a second chance—but at another school."

Several gray areas still exist. One is the responsibility of schools to alert parents if they suspect drug use or if the child seems seriously depressed. In the matter of drug testing of students, too, the verdict is not yet in. The Supreme Court ruled in 1995 that student athletes could be required to submit to random tests, but did not address the question of testing for other students. One major school district did not wait for definitive answers. Routine drug raids at football games that turned up drug vials and led to arrests galvanized the Dade County school system in Florida to institute a six-month pilot program of random drug testing—with parental permission—of all students. Questions have been raised about the possible violation of civil liberties, but it is still too early to know if an avalanche of lawsuits will result. One board member defended the program by saying, "The invasion of privacy is minimal in contrast to the benefit we gain in deterring drug use. Why not do everything we can?"

Parents as well as students have certain rights. If your child is having trouble in school and you feel he or she is not being treated fairly, you have the right to inspect school records and to have a hearing to correct what you think are inaccuracies. Sometimes this right presents school personnel with a dilemma. Does a counselor who is seeing your child have to tell all? Some guidance programs sidestep this privacy question by using informal notes, rather than formal records. These notes do not have to be revealed. This shutting out is hard to accept but may be necessary if your child is to continue to trust the person who is treating him or her.

In order to release records to another person or agency, your written permission or that of the student may be required. Confidentiality also applies if your child is or has been in treatment, and if information is requested by the police. What a teacher or other school employee sees and hears, however, is not part of the formal record and therefore is not protected against disclosure. For instance, if a teacher sees a girl pass a joint of marijuana to another girl in the lunchroom, the teacher may tell the police. Evidence gathered if a student's purse or pockets are searched may also be turned over.

YOUR LEGAL RESPONSIBILITIES

Just as schools have legal responsibilities, so do parents. Some of these rules of law are just rules of common sense. Others are designed to assign accountability. Some hold parents responsible for the actions of their underage children, while others define parental liability for what they themselves do or fail to do.

You are usually responsible:

- If your child damages someone else's property intentionally.

- If your child is selling drugs to kids in your home and you do nothing to stop it. You may be sued by the parents of the buyers.
- If marijuana or other drugs are used on your property. Youngsters in your home are presumed to be your responsibility.
- If your child drives your car while under the influence of alcohol and has his or her driver's license revoked. Your insurance company may cancel your insurance and refuse to renew it.
- If your child drives a car under the influence of alcohol or drugs and has an accident. You may be liable for criminal as well as civil penalties.
- If there is a party at your house and you provide alcohol for minors—or if you are present and do not stop the drinking.
- If a child drinks at the party and then drives and injures someone in an accident.
- If the drinking driver dies.

Even when the youngster is no longer a juvenile, as a "social host" in some states you may be responsible if he drinks too much and then drives. For your own protection (and, of course, for the child's), you should never let a guest at one of your child's parties get into a car and drive if he is under the influence of alcohol or any other drug, no matter how old he is.

Although many legal regulations are tied to legal age, there is one provision that makes it possible to treat someone who is technically a juvenile more like someone who is considerably older. This changes the legal relationship of parent and child. A court can declare a child an "emancipated minor," able to live on his or her own, get whatever social services are available, and be independent of parents. This can be a shocking and devastating blow to parents who have tried to manage a rebellious, drug-using teenager. The mother of a daughter who had been "emancipated" and left home wrote an anguished letter to her local newspaper. "Tell me, who in this world is ready to be on their own at sixteen? Those laws that were made to protect abused children are being used by kids from nice homes who don't want to live by the family rules. The parents don't stand a chance." The irony is that parents may still be financially responsible and required to pay for treatment although they had no choice in the matter. In most states, parents are responsible for their children's financial support until they are adults (usually the age of twenty-one).

AFTER THAT CRITICAL BIRTHDAY

Once your child is no longer a juvenile (has reached the age of sixteen to the age of twenty-one, depending on the state), a crucial line has been crossed. Here are some of the things that will be different:

- When your child is arrested, he may be handcuffed.
- The police (in some states) do not have to contact a parent. (Some youngsters may pay their own fines and never tell their parents they were arrested.)
- Depending on the charge and the circumstances, your child may be held in the local lockup with other prisoners (perhaps overnight) until court is in session.
- Whatever your child says can be used in court.
- Your child may be marked by a criminal record.

Sometimes the changes come as a great shock. Don had been in trouble several times, once for selling pot to his friends and another time for raising hell when he was kept out of a party he was trying to crash. The Juvenile Aid Bureau detective who spoke to him a week before his decisive sixteenth birthday said, "Next time, things won't be this easy." Don assured him he would behave. A week later, his parents were finally forced to face the unpleasant reality when they had to find their way to the holding tank in the police station and see where their son had been locked up overnight.

Deborah Persico, a Washington lawyer dedicated to alerting teenagers to the legal consequences of getting involved with drugs, shocks them by pointing out that even first-time offenders are subject to mandatory prison sentences without parole; that referring a customer to a drug seller or giving a known drug dealer a ride can expose a youngster to prosecution, as can giving a party at which others sell drugs. The teenager who has passed that critical birthday need never have been in trouble before, and need not even have possessed a drug to be charged with a felony that can lead to a long prison sentence.

If you and your child are estranged, you have difficult decisions to make. How much do you want to be involved? Would it be best for your child who is no longer a juvenile to suffer the consequences of his actions? (Keep in mind that he may face a term in state prison rather than a short "shocker" stay in the local lockup.) Can he get his own lawyer? These are judgments only you can make after you have carefully considered the possible penalties and the history of your child's drug use. A term in a state prison is not likely to help a young adult recover from chemical dependency. On the other hand, there comes a time when parents have to detach themselves from their children and let them live their own lives.

Not all cases involve jail or prison terms. Even after children reach their legal age, leniency is possible, particularly for a first offense. The charge may be reduced or the youngster may be treated as a youthful offender, not an adult, at the time of sentencing. This means that his or her name will not appear in the newspapers and that probation (instead of jail or a prison term) may be more likely. Most important of all, as a "youthful offender," he will avoid having a criminal record.

One boy, just seventeen and therefore no longer a minor in New York State, had a few beers and slashed four tires on the car of a girl who had been teasing and tormenting him for three years. His mother says, "It was bizarre. The cops picked up my son as he was driving into the driveway at home. I saw their lights flashing. They weren't even going to tell me."

Since the tires were worth more than $250, this could have been a felony charge, but since it was a first offense, the charge was reduced to a misdemeanor and the boy was put on probation. His probation officer says he doesn't expect him to be in trouble again because "when his friends found out, they told him he was nuts and they wouldn't have let him do it if they'd known."

Like the probation officer, a parent has to look at the total picture and not assume that a child is a substance abuser because of one brush with the law. On the other hand, alcohol and other drugs are usually behind the offenses for which juveniles and young adults are picked up by the police. You can't ignore the possibility that your child is chemically dependent.

When a child is arrested, parents are understandably angry and humiliated. They may be so upset they lash out blindly. Mental health professionals are concerned that even a minor offense can lead to what Cloé Madanes, codirector of the Family Therapy Institute of Washington, calls "such a character assassination that the child feels totally worthless." She recommends that a parent refrain from condemning the child as a person and focus on the fact that the child is still loved. "Society will do the punishing," she says. "The parents don't have to do it."

One of the things that changes most drastically with age is the penalty that can be exacted for a given offense. That's why younger kids are used as runners and sellers for older drug dealers. In Minneapolis, a boy told the local newspaper that one dealer used five youngsters, all under eighteen. "He knew that if we got busted, we got a slap on the hand," the boy said. "If he got it, it was jail for him."

Should you put up bail for your child? According to a probation officer who works with older adolescents (it is rare for a juvenile to be held for bail), each case has to be considered individually. "If this is the first time," she says, "by the time the parent is called, the kid has already been in custody for a while, probably in a holding cell in a police station usually with other people. The kid is already scared enough. You should pay the bail and get him out." But if he is a chronic offender, has already served jail time, and is still breaking the law, "leave him to serve time in a local jail. Sometimes it's the only way to get his attention," she says.

A lawyer who is often appointed by the court to defend youngsters disagrees. "Pay the bail, get him out, at home, and into treatment," she says. "If you don't pay, two things can happen: He can be kept in the local jail with hardened criminals or, if he is young enough, be committed to a youth shelter. Neither is the best place." She points out that bail is designed to ensure that the offender appears in court and doesn't run off; bail isn't a means of punishment. Sometimes a judge wants to teach a youngster a lesson—by saying, "Two or three days in custody will do you good"—but this lawyer disagrees. Often young offenders come out of jail worse than when they went in, and horror stories of rapes and killings are all too true.

For someone who is no longer a juvenile, simple possession of one gram of amphetamines can lead to a sentence of up to a year. Possession of four ounces (113.4 grams) or more of cocaine can carry with it a mandatory sentence of fifteen years to life in a state prison. Possession of just five hundred milligrams (or about five vials) of crack, the concentrated cocaine, can lead to a prison term of from one to seven years. Repeated offenses carry stiffer penalties. And in New York State, where possession of small amounts of marijuana is a nonserious offense akin to a traffic violation, someone who has as much as two ounces is liable to imprisonment for ninety days and/or a $500 fine. In addition, the sale or "gift" of some drugs can result in a mandatory sentence of life imprisonment.

The law also has more subtle provisions. A probation officer in a New York City suburb says, "I warn my own kids that if they're in a car with someone and the car is stopped for a broken headlight and there's pot in the car, if no one owns up to it and it isn't on someone's person, everyone is equally liable. You'd better know who you're riding with and also what they've got with them." A first offense can lead to a $100 fine.

Harsh or helpful, the law is a reality in the lives of many young drug and alcohol abusers. Knowing how it works can help you comprehend what could happen to your child, so that you can help him or her understand, too.

7

Family Fallout

Look at it this way. If someone in the family has a chronic illness, the whole family hurts.

—EILEEN BROWNING,

COFOUNDER AND DIRECTOR, CANDLE (CLARKSTOWN [NEW YORK]

AWARENESS NETWORK FOR A DRUGFREE LIFE AND ENVIRONMENT)

"I always thought we had a good family," the mother of a cocaine-abusing son says. "But then everything fell apart." You may feel that your family, too, is falling apart under the stress of having a drug-abusing child. On the other hand, you may find, as this mother did, that the struggle to achieve a drug-free existence can be a unifying force. "Now that he's been in treatment," she says, "we're closer together than ever." Until that point is reached, families go through hell. Often they react in ways such as these:

- Disrupted rituals. "We always had meals together," a mother says, "but the dinner table became a battlefield. My stomach felt like a pretzel, all twisted up, so I worked it out that Bob ate ahead of time."
- Excessive focus on the addicted child. It's hard to pay attention to anything else when the fear and fighting become monumental. Other children feel lonely and neglected.
- Isolation of the family. Shame and the fear of being criticized make the family pull in on itself. The loneliness can be particularly hard for a single parent.
- Preoccupation with the problem. Families put other parts of their lives aside. A successful stockbroker lost his job because, he says, "I couldn't even remember my own name and telephone number because I was so enmeshed in my daughter's behavior." She was smoking a lot of marijuana, skipping school, and acting up at home. "At one point," he adds, "I actually contemplated suicide just to get out of the family situation."

MARRIAGE

As a child's love affair with drugs progresses, the parents' relationship goes through different stages too, from disbelief, to worry, to a recognition of the reality and feelings of anger, terror, and helplessness. By the time a child has been seduced by alcohol or drug use, parents may be constantly at odds. One denies the problem, the other recognizes it. Or both continue to feel that something is wrong but never connect the trouble to the same cause. Even when the problem's origins are clear, dissension may persist. Blaming is part of the game.

When an Ohio couple found out their son was addicted to heroin, "it was catastrophic. My husband cried all week-end. We were both furious with each other. We were both convinced the other 'had done it'! The blaming didn't last long, but it was blazing."

Their therapist told them, "You need to stay together and work together to get through this," and they did. They realized that their resentments of each other went way back—"He was always too lenient with the kid"; "She's an off-the-wall mother"—and probably had little to do with drug abuse. "And," the mother says, "we came to see that maybe it was his fault, maybe mine, maybe nobody's—whatever. We've got to deal with it."

Counselors say that blame, guilt, and shame are the common trilogy of feelings when parents confront a child's drug abuse. The vast majority of parents blame the other parent and are filled with helpless rage. "I couldn't fix my kid," one mother says, "so I was mad at my husband because he couldn't do it and my drug-using kid was mad at himself because he couldn't do it either." All this anger spills over into arguments, fights, and constant turmoil.

Some adolescents reinforce the discord and are what one counselor calls "professional parent-splitters." One marriage survived this ploy because the parents made an agreement: "If we knew we didn't have consensus," the father says, "we'd say, 'We'll tell you our answer in our own good time.' Then we'd talk it over alone first, and whoever had the harder line won."

Some marriages fall apart under the stress, while others get stronger. "My marriage almost pulled apart," one mother remembers. "My husband and my other kids thought it was all my fault. Then, when our daughter went into treatment, we had to go into a parents' group. My husband didn't want to have anything to do with it, but he said he'd go 'just this once.' "

During the session, they cried because life had gotten so dismal. Finally, they admitted that they both secretly hoped their daughter would never come home from the treatment center so they could go on fantasizing that life could be as before.

After the three-hour group meeting, they were drained. "We put our arms around each other, both crying, and felt closer than we'd felt in years," the mother says. Their daughter has been in aftercare now for two years and both her parents are recovering along with her.

THE DIVORCED FAMILY

Youngsters are even more likely to drive a wide wedge between their parents if the parents are already separated. They know who is the easy touch and ask things of that person. They play on fear ("I can always go live with him") and guilt ("If you hadn't left, this wouldn't have happened"). But, as with other important decisions about a child's life, parents have to get together and agree on how to handle the situation. The agreement doesn't have to be monolithic— differences are inevitable—but basics such as rules concerning drug and alcohol use should be the same. Once in a while, playing musical families—running from one to the other—can be helpful rather than hurtful. The child may use the time away from one parent as a cooling-off period, and then be able to come back with a different perspective.

Sometimes, however, parental cooperation just isn't possible. The divorced mother of three children, two of whom got involved in drugs, says, "They had a father very anxious to corrupt his kids to get even with his wife. He used to offer them drugs when they came to visit." All a parent can do under these circumstances is to try some innovative solutions—curtail visits, go back to court, plan trips, move farther away. If one parent has remarried and the child lives with the remarried parent, the situation may be unusually touchy. Although a stepfather went reluctantly to Nar-Anon meetings with his wife, he kept saying, "We don't have problems like other people here. It's not drugs. He's just a lousy kid." Of course it was drugs, and the mother felt her husband, who had never had children of his own, didn't understand and expected too much of his two stepsons.

The stepson soon developed a manipulative technique for diverting attention from himself. "If we tried to talk to him about what he was doing, he would maneuver us into an argument with each other and then slip out the back door." This mother says that as her marriage began to show the strain, "I knew I had to make it clear that he wasn't going to come between us. He would be grown up and gone and I'd still want the marriage."

Sometimes parents and stepparents use their child as a scapegoat. They argue about the child's problems and avoid their own. It's easier to say, "Everything is his fault," instead of looking at dissatisfaction with each other. Parental tensions have to be faced or the treatment of the child will have a hard time succeeding. As one family therapist puts it, "If your child has a problem, you have a problem."

THE DENYING SPOUSE

When you see the problem and your spouse doesn't, what do you do? A family therapist says, "It's almost impossible to find a time in the crisis when the two of you are in the same place," but you don't have to let being out of step stymie you. Instead of being immobilized until you reach agreement, you can get help for yourself. You can't change the other person, but you can change the way you relate to that person.

One mother was distraught because her sixteen-year-old was getting high on marijuana and not showing up at school. Her husband's reaction was: "If you wouldn't make such a big deal of this, everything would be fine." In desperation, the mother joined a self-help group. "I didn't have my husband with me. I didn't have my kid in treatment— but I regained my sanity," she says. After a few meetings, she was able to talk to her husband without seeming hysterical, and he began to realize that their daughter really was cutting school in order to use drugs and their younger children were at risk. The family is now in treatment.

THE OTHER CHILDREN

No simple way exists to keep the addicted child from contaminating the other children in the family. Studies show that many youngsters who are users were introduced to drugs by an older brother or sister. You should recognize that your other children are at greater-than-normal risk of becoming users themselves if one child is a drug abuser. Do everything you can to help them feel competent and worthwhile so they will be less tempted. "Catch them being good," says a counselor. "Honest praise and recognition are the best vaccine."

When a family is in turmoil because of a drug-abusing child, the other children try desperately to keep the family on course. They often play one or more of these roles:

- The grown-up who takes over duties and responsibilities beyond his years because his parents are too preoccupied or demoralized to function well.
- The peacemaker who steps in to defuse tense situations and protect the drug user from an angry parent, or a parent from the irrational or combative user.
- The policeman who acts as a detective and reports on the activities of the user.
- The protector who embodies the family's denial that anything serious is going on, and struggles with divided loyalties as he keeps his knowledge of his brother's or sister's drug use from his parents.
- The perfect child who tries to do everything right and make up to the parents for the failures and disappointments they face with the other child.
- The carbon copy who does everything the drug-abusing brother or sister did at the same age, joining the same kind of crowd, getting into the same difficulties, and re-creating a familiar family pattern.

It's important that you talk to your other children about the feelings that are pushing them into taking these roles. The family has to recognize that all of its members are in pain, and you have to make it clear that this is something that can be discussed.

For instance, if one of your children is playing the perfect child, that child is carrying all the weight of the hope that was once spread around. The model child hides any negative feelings and tries desperately to live up to expectations. Some youngsters say, "I had to give up what I really was, to be what my parents needed me to be. I had to be a source of pleasure rather than of upset." This is a hard way to live. One therapist suggests that you say to your children in one way or another, "You have your own lives. You're not responsible for our happiness. We know that with all our attention on your brother or sister, you have, in a way, lost us. And we understand that this hurts." Just the open recognition of the strains and permission to talk about them can help ease the need to play a certain role.

Even young children are affected. The child knows something is wrong, but doesn't know what it is. If Mom yells "Why can't you be quiet?" the child thinks the trouble exists because of something he or she did. Here, too, the best way to handle the upset is to explain what is going on—in different ways for different ages. If your child is just six years old, you might have to start at the beginning and explain the basics of what a drug is and what it does to thinking and behavior.

"No matter how old or young they are," says a school counselor, "if they ask you what's going on, you'd better tell them. They know something isn't right, and honest answers are better than fiction." You can help them see that when people talk about addiction, they're talking about a disease, and a person can't stop using even if he wants to stop hurting other people. This can help them if they are taunted in school with "Your brother's a druggie." If the "druggie" is in treatment, the rejoinder can be "My brother's sick and he's getting help." If he is still using, you can say to your other child, "It sounds like you feel miserable when you go to school. You're worried and we're worried, too, and we have to decide what to do." Accepting the nonusing child's feelings is at least a beginning.

Worry is only one of the feelings other children in a family struggle with. Some of them feel guilt—a kind of "survivor's guilt"—because they are well and their brother or sister is not. Some feel guilty because they first "turned on" the user. Your other children may also feel they did or said something to precipitate what happened if serious drug use, suicide attempts, or running away occur. They may need professional help. Sometimes their emotions are so strong that, if they are old enough, they leave home feeling, "I don't want to have anything to do with this anymore."

Younger children feel frightened and vulnerable and may be subjected to violent outbursts from the drug user. If they are left in the care of a stoned sibling, the dangers are very real. One little girl told her teacher that her brother went to sleep every afternoon after school when he was supposed to be looking after her. If your older child can't be counted on, you have to enlist the help of someone else to oversee the household when you can't be at home.

If your drug-using child is physically abusing the younger children or involving them in his or her drug life, you will have serious and difficult decisions to make. Don't try to make them alone. Get help from someone you respect—a clergyman, counselor, therapist—or from a self-help group. If the situation is critical, turn to the law. (See Chapter 6.)

One single mother called the police when her son became enraged and out of control and started kicking his younger sister with his cowboy boots. But despite the terrible times they had together, and despite the fact that he has lived away from home for several years, "it didn't destroy family ties," his mother says. This boy's brother and sister still keep in touch with him. His brother, like many children who have grown up in families with problems, has had in-house training in helping others and is now studying to be a social worker.

Even when the family seems completely torn apart, don't give up. Tom's older brother, a very straight senior in college, said of his crack-using brother, "The best thing that could happen would be if he was picked up by the police." He wanted to have nothing to do with him. When Tom went into treatment, his mother told the brother that this was a time Tom really needed the family around. His brother said nothing and seemed unresponsive. Yet, to everyone's surprise, he visited Tom while he was in treatment and even sent him a birthday card.

GRANDPARENTS AND OTHERS

In addition to brothers and sisters, other people come into the picture. Grandparents can be very shocked when they learn that an adored grandchild is smoking cigarettes or using drugs. You have to tread easily with these older people, but they often need to know the truth even though they may file it away in a part of the brain that doesn't get looked at often.

One woman said the most difficult time for her was a Christmas celebration at her parents' house that had traditionally involved wine for everyone. Her daughter had recently been discharged after three months in a rehabilitation facility, and there was to be no alcohol in any place she visited. The woman was faced with telling her own mother that this year they would all have to forgo the wine in deference to the girl's needs. The mother was ashamed of what had happened to her daughter and had been tempted to keep up the denial until her daughter made it clear she would not come to dinner unless her grandmother was informed. You may be tempted to take the seemingly easy, silent way out with other relatives, too, but it is often not the best way.

Then there are friends and neighbors who will be curious. "Where's Danny these days?" "Where does Mary go? We don't see her around anymore."

Whether you are dealing with grandparents, other relatives, friends, or neighbors, those who work with drug- and alcohol-abusing youngsters say you should:

- Be honest—or at least as honest as you can be. One woman didn't tell her ninety-year-old mother who lived in another town "because it would destroy her." But if there are no health restrictions, openness is best. For family sanity, the more the broad outlines are known, the easier it will be. Says a California mother, "I'm handling my parents the same way I handle my friends. I find the more open I am, the more responsive they are."
- Be clear that help (if asked for) is welcome, but interference is not.
- Be prepared for a rocky shakedown period. Some people will be understanding, some will not. A woman told a

dinner-table companion about her son and was told, "If he was my son, I'd bash his head through the wall." You will discover who stands by you in adversity.

- Be proud if your child is going for help. If you are ashamed, how can your child feel good about the difficult, constructive steps he is taking?

Even if your child is not in treatment, your openness can make a difference. Relatives who know what's going on can be valuable backups. As one couple literally pushed their son out the door after he had repeatedly refused to stop using drugs, they said, "You can't come home. But you can call Uncle George." Then they changed the locks on the front door. The boy did call his uncle within a week and said he was ready for treatment. Then the uncle called the parents, saying, "Don't be surprised and don't yell or scream. We're bringing him back." The uncle had succeeded where the parents could not.

Relatives are not always this supportive. Old wounds and rivalries are sometimes reawakened when a family's mythical view of itself is shaken. "The rest of the family does a marvelous tiptoe act," says the mother of a drug-abusing son. Her husband is one of eight children who had an alcoholic father. "I tell my sisters-in-law that their kids have as much of a chance of being hooked as mine. But they really don't want to know."

Grandparents, too, may deny or may use this situation as a way to continue old patterns. One mother who had always been critical of her daughter said, "How could you be such a lousy parent?" And when her grandson was in treatment, "How could you send him to that terrible place?" She was critical of her grandchild, too. There are times when it is best to stay out of firing range until you are better able to deal with attacks such as these.

PARENTS AS PEOPLE

Emotions are intensified when there is a crisis in the family. A mother may be so attached to her child that she cannot disentangle herself enough to see what must be done. Despite the fact that she knew from personal experience with an alcoholic husband that Al-Anon's philosophy of detachment was helpful, one mother said, "It's different with my daughter. I conceived her, carried her, birthed her, nursed her, and raised her. I cannot think of her apart from me. When she hurts, I hurt."

This intense bond may produce a family triangle—mother and child allied against the father. A father who feels like an outsider may turn his hurt feelings into anger. Fighting—physical and verbal—is often part of the picture. One father felt his son was irresponsible, lying, and "filthy-mouthed." "Once I broke my finger separating them," recalls the mother. "I always blamed my husband for the trouble." Later, she understood that her husband had hated himself for the way he treated his son, but he felt powerless in his family.

It is often the parent of the opposite sex who stands up for the drug user and the parent of the same sex who is harsh, as it was in this case. "It's almost like [emotional] incest," says the father of a drug abuser who mapped the responses in his parent support group, referring to the emotional protectiveness of mother for son and father for daughter (rather than to physical or sexual contact).

It isn't easy, but you will all be better off if you can see that although you care for your child, you can't carry the burden of pain for him or her. And if both parents stand together, the child and the family have a better chance of recovering.

8

Grown-up Children, Puzzled Parents

Our children will be our children for the rest of our lives, and sometimes that's not fair.

—BILL COSBY

No matter how good your intentions, giving advice to an adult child can be problematic. When a counselor asked one mother if she had ever tried to talk to her twenty-eight-year-old son about his drinking, she said, "No. He wouldn't have listened." The son, who was also being interviewed, added, "I would have told you to shut up and go to hell."

You, too, may be told, "It's none of your business." "Children" in their twenties, thirties, and forties who are involved with drugs and/or alcohol present parents with an agonizing dilemma. Often they are out in the world and on

155

their own. At this point you may feel, "I've done my job. Now it's their turn." And yet, as Dr. Margaret M. Lawrence, a well-known child psychiatrist, points out, "You are always a parent." This means that you want—and often try—to help.

Before you say anything, you should have some evidence that a problem really exists. Some adult children who use drugs started using as teenagers. Others may have escaped the epidemic until they were in college or at work, and you may have to decide if the changes you see are indications of drug use or just a response to unaccustomed freedom.

No certainties exist, but there are warning flags you can watch out for, whether your child is away at college, living on his own, living with a friend, married, or still at home. The basic indicator is a discrepancy between what he or she says and what is really happening. If "I'm fine" doesn't fit with the messed-up life you see or hear about, you should take a closer look. Specific drugs also have particular warning signs (see Chapter 3). Look or listen for general danger signals such as:

- Problems with money. Asking for gifts or loans; not repaying debts. Repeated plaintive phone calls—"My car needs fixing again"—or blatant attempts to acquire extra cash.
- Problems with housing. Sudden need for a mortgage, the loss of a home, or overdue rent. A neglected or messy apartment or a run-down house. Eviction notices. Here, too, money is the key.
- Problems at work. Losing job after job. Moving from place to place for work. Poor job performance, including

arguments with coworkers or supervisors. Unexplained absences caused by alcoholism or drug use can derail a career.

- Difficulties at home. Complaints from a partner or spouse. Arguments, physical fights. Marital breakup, child abuse, and neglect.
- Changes in sleep patterns. Nodding; short daytime naps. Reversal of day/night cycle, staying up all night and sleeping all day. Some drugs put people to sleep while others put them into high gear.
- Changes in personal looks and neatness. Dramatic weight loss (eating becomes secondary when life focuses on the drug); unrepaired, unsightly teeth; unkempt appearance and infrequent bathing.
- Changes in attitudes. Excuses for being late, not carrying through on promises. No motivation. Suspiciousness of parents, friends, teachers, or coworkers.
- Drop in academic performance. Lower grades, incompletes. This is probably the best indicator for college students.
- Changes in behavior. Temper outbursts. Frequent trips to the bathroom, basement, garage, or other secluded areas. Inability to carry on a coherent conversation.

Sometimes it is very hard to come up with unmistakable evidence. A twenty-two-year-old who was using heroin hid his habit successfully from both his parents and his doctor. Instead of injecting himself along his arms and legs as addicts usually do, he used the veins on the tops of his feet. Despite the difficulties, you shouldn't make the mistake of waiting for the "smoking gun." At some point, you will have to decide whether to confront your child, and whether your jumping in will help him more than it will hurt you. Consider these questions, too:

- How old is your child? How responsible do you feel for him or her?
- What other supports—spouse, friends—does he or she have?
- How destructive is the drug or alcohol use in terms of the potential for self-destruction or harm to others?
- How much energy do you have—or want—to expend? Are there other children at home who need you, too?
- How much money can you—or will you—spend for help or treatment?
- Does your child want you involved at all?
- Do you really want to try to help at this point, or have you had it?

If you decide that you want to try to do something, timing is extremely important. Just as with a younger child, don't try to talk if the person is high. Dr. Richard Rawson of the Matrix Center in Beverly Hills, an outpatient clinic for drug users, suggests the best time to bring up the subject of cocaine use is at lunch on Monday when the user will be in a post-cocaine depression. Friday night is the worst time—he's all geared up to go out. The same timing is valid for other drugs, too.

During your conversation, don't attack or accuse. Dr. Rawson suggests you express concern and love, and explore several hypotheses to explain the behavior you have noticed. You might ask, "Are you upset about a relationship? Are you having trouble on your job?" and then go on: "I've read a lot about coke [or alcohol abuse] and I wonder if you see any of this." You can expect some denial: "Yeah, some of my friends use it, but I've never gotten involved," or "I've tried it a few times." Once you are convinced your child is hiding the truth, you should carefully consider what options you have to influence his or her behavior. As the mother of a multiple drug user put it, "To a kid you can say, 'Don't run in the street,' or 'Don't touch the stuff under the sink.' But to a twenty-six-year-old, you can't say what to do."

Nevertheless, those who work with alcohol and drug abusers say you often do have some power and some options. For example, money can be withheld unless certain conditions are met; your relationship with your child can be placed on the line. A child away from home (at college, for instance) can be brought home, or one at home can be kicked out (this is a last resort). Which options you can use and when you use them depend a lot on how close you and your child are, geographically and emotionally.

CHILDREN IN COLLEGE

A child who lives at a university or a college presents a special case. He is temporarily out of the house and yet you're responsible for him. You're probably paying the bills, and have some concern about turning your kid loose in a world that is full of hazards.

One girl went wild with her college freedom and was forced by her parents to return home. She protested, but she did it. When she had calmed down and was removed from her drug- and alcohol-using friends, she began to study. She obviously hadn't been ready to be on her own.

In another case, even saying "If your grades don't improve, you will have to come home and go to school here" didn't end the drug use. A mother says, "We had him come back. I would listen to those commercials that ask, 'Do you know where your children are?' and then answer, 'Yes.' I knew John and his girlfriend were in the family room. I didn't know they were shooting heroin."

That may be an extreme case, but trying to reach out and influence your almost adult son or daughter is always tricky, as one Chicago mother realized when she got a weepy phone call from her freshman son. Although his parents had divorced when he was in junior high school, he had gotten through the rocky early teens without too much trouble. But here he was, slurring his words and crying and talking long distance for two hours. "I never told Dad I loved him before he split. I haven't told you how much I love you," he kept repeating. His mother was afraid that in his drunken state he was thinking of suicide. She tried to reassure him, but hasn't had the courage to talk about the drinking or alert the school. "If the school calls him in and he knows I tipped them off, I'll lose him," she says.

Yet you can approach the situation in ways that work. A college physician suggests that if parents are worried, they say to their son or daughter, "What can I do to help you? I'm so far away—would it be okay with you if we contact the dean of students or a counselor so we can get help for you?" Align yourself with the child, she says, and don't do anything behind his or her back. You can say you know that there are people on campus who deal with things like this every day, and who really understand young people. "And don't neglect college chaplains as a source," she suggests.

A call to school authorities is most likely to have some

effect if your child is at a small school, but at a huge university, "they couldn't care less and probably wouldn't follow through," according to Dr. Rodney Skager of UCLA. You will have to provide the pressure. "If you suspect drug or alcohol use because your kid is having other problems—academic ones, for instance—focus on these problems," he says, "in order not to raise his defenses." If your child won't go for counseling on his own, you may have to travel to the campus to investigate private therapists in the area or the school counseling services to select someone for him. Alert the counselor in advance by saying something like "I think drugs are involved. Maybe you can do something," but point out that your child will be coming ostensibly because of other problems. And you can tell your child, "Let's not argue about whether you could use some help. Let's let a trained counselor decide."

If your child still refuses to go for help, Dr. Skager says, "you'd better have some sanctions ready." One father told his son, "You have three choices—the army, the navy, or the marines." Other parents have said "no car" or "no tuition" or used other financial pressures.

Although some parents call the college and try to get a child into treatment, it is more common for the school to call the parents, particularly if there is an emergency. "When we call with the student's permission," a counselor at an eastern college says, "parents don't believe it and don't believe someone that young could be addicted. Some eventually come around, some never do. Most of them say, 'You're exaggerating. It's just a phase.'"

If your child runs into a crisis, the first thing you must do, of course, is to take it seriously. Often it's hard to believe that a young person who has functioned well enough to get through high school and into college would suddenly be unable to handle the new pressures to use alcohol or drugs. But the doctor who treated a girl who talked to squirrels on campus while she was hallucinating put it this way: "She had a pin holding things together. LSD took the pin out and she fell apart." Although she had seemed fine, she was hiding a lot behind the successful exterior. For a whole year the children in her family had to pass notes back and forth from one parent to the other because they weren't talking to each other, although they continued to live under the same roof.

This doesn't mean that every youngster who has a bad trip, drinks too much, or is hooked on pills comes from a family with serious problems. It does mean that if something like this happens to your child, you have to be willing to look at your family life and your personal life as well as your child. You won't be able to understand your child's problems without understanding your own.

If your child has had to drop out of college because of drug use (or never made it that far), should you pay tuition if she wants to go back (or start)? If she has stopped using (on her own or with treatment) and you can afford to help, counselors say she should be given the same kind of support you would have given earlier, with this proviso: If drug use starts again, tuition ends. One single parent took a second mortgage on her house to pay her son's tuition. Another parent says, "If you make the assumption the whole thing is a disease, and he's working a program and trying to come to terms with his addiction, of course you'll help him go to school." She points out that the "stoned years" were a true gap, and that life doesn't pick up again until the drug use ends. "Even my goody-goody nephew has a gap in his education—he took a year off," she says. "So it's not unusual these days. People frequently take years off."

LIVING AWAY FROM HOME

You have some ways to influence your college-age child, but the young adult who is living independently can be harder to reach. What's more, you may be more conflicted about whether it will be worth the effort. The father of a thirty-year-old who has been involved with drugs since his early teens puts it this way: "Often when I don't hear from him for a while, I'm frightened because I'm sure he's dead—overdosed. But sometimes I actually feel I don't particularly give a damn. I don't really know him anymore. Since he was seventeen, I haven't seen him much."

Despite these feelings, this father, like most parents, still wants the best for his child, still wants him to recover, still wants him to have a good life.

If you continue to provide gifts or support, you can say to your child, "Until you do something about your drinking or drug-taking, I won't pay for car insurance, or rent, or doctor bills." Then you can offer to help find the right treatment, pay for it (if you can afford it and haven't been forced to do it again and again), and provide whatever emotional support you can.

The father of a young woman who drank too much and also "was seeing six doctors and getting drugs from twelve pharmacies" did just this. He was able to convince her to go to a hospital for detoxification after a formal intervention. (See page 178.) Curiously, once she was drug-free and scheduled to go into long-term inpatient treatment, she balked. She felt she could make it on her own. For the first time her father, who helped pay the rent for her apartment, threatened her: "If you don't go in, you've gotten your last penny from me." The threat worked, he says, because "it was said as coldly as possible, so she was sure I wouldn't back off." She is now working, paying her own way, and off all drugs, including alcohol.

Perhaps you have tried to use the power of the purse strings and failed. Then you may have no power left except that of your relationship. After supporting and then refusing to support their thirty-year-old heroin-using son, paying intermittently for tuition when he hardly ever went to classes and having him bounce in and out of their home, the parents came to a painful decision. Their son was serving a term in jail ("for dealing, I think"), and they let him know that the only thing they would do was pick him up when he was released and drive him to an inpatient treatment center. If he rejected their offer, they would no longer have direct contact with him.

They now communicate only through a third person. They refuse to talk on the phone and refuse to receive or write letters. The last word they had was that he wanted his skis. Instead of letting him come home for them, they left them at a neighbor's house. He never showed up. "It's awful and it hasn't worked, but at least we feel we're trying something," his mother says. "And we are less helpless, less enmeshed in his life, and in less turmoil."

Dealing with an unmarried adult child is one thing, but when your child is married, complications are compounded. If you disagree with your son- or daughter-in-law about drug use, you could be faced with gigantic fights. At the same time, if you agree, you can work together. First you must consider these questions:

- Are you close enough to your son or daughter and his or her spouse to talk easily?
- Will they tell you exactly what is going on?
- Can you help without making anyone feel inadequate?

The mother of a son who had been drinking heavily and secretly for ten years was able to be a real help to him and to his family by providing the backing they needed without criticizing or blaming. When he called her and said drunkenly, "Your son is a bum. I'm an alcoholic," she countered, "You're not a bum. We'll get help."

She and her daughter-in-law went with him to an Alcoholics Anonymous meeting that morning. The next evening, when they all went again, he took a bottle of vodka with him. An AA member said, "You can come in, but you can't bring that in," and he threw it away. That was his last drink. When he hesitated to enter a twenty-eight-day rehabilitation program because of the time and the money, his mother said, "The kids can always stay at my house. Don't worry. They'll be fed." And she began occasionally to accompany his wife to Al-Anon meetings.

Grandchildren can profit from a close relationship with their grandparents at times like these. They may need extra attention, baby-sitting, or the fun of going to the zoo. Just talking to them or letting them talk to you can be helpful. Consider carefully whether it is your business to talk to them about their parent's use of chemicals. If you are a "visiting" grandparent, the subject may not come up. Children have often been told not to talk to anyone about it, not even Grandma. But if you see these children often, they are apt to ask a question or say, "I don't like Mama when she's drinking." Then a straight answer from you is the only one. Tell the child what alcohol or any drug does to thinking and point out that the parent's behavior is the result of the action of the drug on the brain. The parent is not bad and does not intend to be mean. And, most important, make sure the child understands and really believes that it is not his fault that his parent is drinking too much or using drugs.

COMING HOME TO VISIT

If your drug-using child comes to visit, he should be asked to leave if he's high or drunk when he arrives. If he protests, tell him you'd like to spend time with him, but only when he is sober or more in control of himself. He'll get the message when you let him know that it's no fun for you or anyone else to have him around when he really isn't functioning. Be prepared for an angry response, but try not to give in. Your child must learn to suffer the full consequences of his behavior.

Many parents ask, "What should I do if my son lights up a joint while he's visiting us?" First of all, be clear about your convictions before an incident occurs. If you'd rather your child didn't hide the fact that he or she is using pot, make this plain. If such use is unacceptable to you, then you must say so unequivocally. You can point out that it is illegal, adding, "We enjoy your visits, but not your smoking."

A woman who had smoked pot herself in the sixties put it this way to her daughter: "I can't control what you do.

But this is my house, and the bottom line is I won't have it around." You can use the same approach when it comes to other drugs. You have to be prepared for tension and even an angry "Well, then, I won't visit anymore."

WHEN HARM THREATENS

At times, visits with a drug-using child present a real danger. Many drugs reduce inhibitions and allow people to act on their wishes or impulses. Angry, embittered people who feel thwarted by society use drugs not only to "nod out" but to "act out."

A young man who had been living on the streets of New York showed up at home to ask his parents for money. They knew he would use it to buy drugs, and they refused. But then he said, "If you don't give it to me, I'll burn the house down." They knew he was serious, and that the threat was a real one, and they did what he asked.

The threat is sometimes against the addict. One "pothead" told his parents that he had sold $125 worth of marijuana as an agent for someone else, and had not turned over the money. The dealer was threatening to "break both his legs." Here, too, his parents acceded to the extortion, fearing what might happen. Theoretically, it would have been best to let him face the consequences, but theory and real life often conflict.

If you feel your grown child poses a real threat or danger to himself or to others, you are going to have to alert the police, a trustworthy friend, or some emergency facility, no matter what his age or where he lives. Otherwise lives—even your own—might be in jeopardy. If he menaces you,

you can get a court order to keep him away. If he is a threat to public safety (as an airline pilot, bus driver, or railroad engineer, for example), you have a responsibility to report him to an appropriate authority. If you feel your child is a threat to his or her own life, you cannot stand by and do nothing. A twenty-four-year-old active alcoholic came home and confessed that she was considering suicide. Her mother pointed out she had made this threat many times and it hadn't meant a thing. The parents ignored her plea for help, and the next day, the young woman jumped off the Golden Gate Bridge. Suicide threats should always be taken seriously. (See page 69.)

Other indications of trouble may be less direct. Your child's friends may say things like "George looks really wasted. I'm worried. Is he all right?" This, too, should be taken seriously. Your visits or glimpses into your independent child's life can provide clues that can't be picked up in phone conversations. Then you will have to decide if you want to do more.

COMING HOME TO LIVE

You probably felt reasonably sure that when your son or daughter left for college or moved away, your household would be your own. It's a real shock when this child, for whatever reason, turns up on your doorstep and expects to be welcomed back. Today, many adults are returning home for financial reasons, sometimes bringing all their worldly goods and their families, too. Many come home because drugs have caught up with them and they have no place else to go.

One cocaine-addicted young man came home to his parents after his wife threw him out. The son asked for money, the use of the car, and a place to stay "until I find a job." Even though he had done this before, his parents' first impulse was to accept him, but they steeled themselves, finally realizing that the most helpful thing they could do was to say no. They let him know that they considered him an adult and would no longer support him even though they were on his side, and that he could no longer lean on them.

If your grown child is still part of the drug scene and wants to move in, the answer should be a definite no. You're only helping the illness to progress if you supply shelter on demand. As an alternative, you can help him or her find a job or housing elsewhere with the understanding that treatment begin at the same time. If you give in and allow this adult child to infringe on your rights, you and the others with whom you live are in for a lot of strife.

If your child is in treatment or has completed treatment and needs a secure haven in which to recover, the situation is different. Providing comfort and love and reducing financial pressures can make a difference in the long-term outcome. But adjustments must be made on both sides.

If you have a good relationship with your recovering child and are afraid to rock the boat, you will still need to talk about what happened so the child doesn't transmit the illness to the next generation and you can get rid of some of your own hostile feelings. "You will live less scared," said one counselor.

Alice is an only child who used drugs and alcohol for a decade and finally went into a hospital for treatment "that worked" when she was twenty-seven years old. She had lived in another part of the country for years but now lives at home and says, "I think about what stupid things I did. How I hurt my parents. A lot of things I didn't want to do, I want to do now—staying home, cooking dinner."

Her parents are still protective. "It takes every ounce of strength they've got not to say, 'Where are you going? When will you be back?' " But, she says, "I tell them, 'You can't do everything for me.' " Alice has a part-time job, and resists suggestions that she work full-time because she isn't ready for that. She's learned to speak up. "It's amazing how childlike you can get when you talk to your parents," she says, "and how different it is when you talk adult to adult."

STILL AT HOME

Some adult children never move out. But letting an adult drug user live at home, particularly when younger children are present, can lead to nothing but disaster. "When you support him, you're supporting his habit. If he's legally of age, the time to cut the strings is now," says the mother of a boy who smoked marijuana daily and was addicted to alcohol. He lived at home until he was almost thirty. "It wasn't easy. My own mother said, 'How can you kick him out?' " she recalls. "I told her I didn't kick him out, I didn't say, 'leave,' I said, 'Stop using, or get into treatment—or leave.' " These parents feel they were helped to maintain their stance through participation in a Toughlove group. (See page 109.)

People who work with drug and alcohol abusers point out that parents who feel they cannot ask their children to leave should certainly make clear-cut demands. With the help of a support group, one mother finally had the courage to tell her thirty-one-year-old son that if he wanted to stay at home, he would have to pay room and board. Otherwise, as a group member pointed out, "You're leaving him free to use the money he earns to buy drugs." After a few months of contributing to the household, he joined the navy—an intermediate step to living completely on his own.

LETTING GO

Separating is part of parenting, and the time must come, early for some, later for others, to loosen the grip so the child can grow up. At a certain point, you are no longer responsible for your child's life, debts, or the consequences of his or her behavior.

This letting go should be gentle. A parent does not have to abandon the child or drop him with a thud—no matter how old he is. Letting go means gentle release, with love, perhaps even support of one kind or another.

If the addiction continues or keeps recurring, you must realize that no matter what you do, you cannot make the difference. A New York psychotherapist tells parents of adults who are hooked on cocaine or crack to view the addiction as a terminal disease. "It follows an inexorable course and we really don't know how to deal with it very well," he says. "If parents can see it this way, they aren't so bitter and they can accept their own helplessness. They can also understand the helplessness of their child."

Even when things aren't this bad, parents often hold on too long. It's almost a reflex action to try to protect the twenty-nine-year-old as you did the nine-year-old. A successful lawyer views with amused tolerance his mother who still asks him each time they're about to get into the car for a long ride, "Do you want to go to the bathroom, dear?"

If you are still too deeply immersed in the problems of your drug-using child, you have to decide just how much you can or should do. If you can't persuade or threaten your child into getting help, you can still disengage and get help for yourself. This sends several messages. One is that you care. Another is that you are not defeated by life. For a young adult who feels helpless and defeated by the power of drug addiction, your behavior can provide a powerful model. Even if your grown-up "kid" is not talking to you, you remain a special person in his life, and it's important for him to know he is not destroying you and you believe human beings can change. This can give him hope that there is a chance for him, too.

For no clear reason, many adolescents and young people grow out of certain behaviors, including the use of psychoactive drugs. Certain ages bring certain behaviors with them, and just as the rebellious two-year-old grows naturally out of the no-saying years, the rebellious adolescent grows out of his perilous risk-taking. If he makes it to the age of thirty, he may also grow out of excessive consumption of alcohol and, perhaps, other drugs. This has been true of many of the young people who used marijuana in the fifties and sixties. Many stopped with very little or no prodding and without professional help. Marriage often makes the difference. A 1997 study by researchers at the University of Michigan showed that marijuana use dropped by more than one-third and cocaine use dropped by one-half after young adults got married.

Dr. David Smith, founder and director of the Haight-Ashbury Free Clinic in San Francisco, says, "We have done interviews with a nonabuse population. A significant number report that marijuana was a phase in their lives and say that the alternative to use is not necessarily treatment, but some other drug-free phase. They have given up drugs on their own and are now committed to good nutrition, the peace movement, and rearing families." He says also that in general, kids who experiment grow out of it; kids who become addicted do not, and may get worse as they get older.

Since there's no telling what the long run may hold for your particular child (and the popularity of and easy access to crack and methamphetamine have made addiction much more likely than it was in the sixties), you cannot dismiss your child's drug use as a phase.

THE LONG VIEW

Your adult child may not grow out of drug use and may rebuff your efforts to help or ask only that you be the one who gives, offering nothing in return. It's hard not to just turn your back and give up. Even if your relationship with your child hasn't been good for a long time, don't think it's ever too late to correct it, even at age twenty, thirty, or forty. Sometimes the most you can do is keep yourself available by saying, "I'm here, and when you decide to straighten out your life, I'll still be here."

9

Finding the Right Help

I've seen kids recover that I wouldn't have bet a plugged nickel
on. Everyone has a chance.

—AN INPATIENT DRUG COUNSELOR

Once you've faced reality and know that your child
needs help, the big task lies ahead. You must find out
what kind of help would be best for your particular child,
and what is available close to home. You may not know
where to turn first. You can begin by using your local phone
book. In the yellow pages, counseling services and hotlines
are usually listed under Alcoholism Treatment or Drug
Abuse Information and Treatment. In the white pages of
phone books in and around large cities, you will find a listing under Community Services Numbers or in the directory
in the front of the book. Other possibilities listed below

will have entries in the white pages. Start with a call to one or more of these:

- Your family doctor.
- An agency specializing in treating drug/alcohol abuse and related problems (often listed in the yellow pages under Drug Abuse).
- A local counseling or mental health center.
- A community-based storefront counseling center.
- A physician, social worker, psychologist, or drug counselor.
- An emergency hotline.
- The school guidance department or student assistance service.
- A police youth officer.
- A clergyman.
- A relative you trust, particularly one in a helping profession.

After you've talked to several people and found out who works well with children, adolescents, and families and is experienced with substance abuse, make an appointment. Don't let your child or anyone else change your mind, belittle your convictions, or make you believe you are an alarmist. If you are blowing the situation out of proportion, a counselor will soon let you know.

Some parents prefer to talk on the phone to a counselor before making an appointment. Others are more comfortable face-to-face. But no matter how or where your first contact occurs, you need to get your facts straight—in writing, if necessary—before the interview. Focus on what is happening in your family—the family history, drug-abuse history—and what you want to find out. Many parents are so distraught when they finally realize their child is messing up his life, they become confused. One mother lost the car keys as she was getting ready to leave for an appointment she had made a week earlier with the trusted family doctor. When she got to him, she couldn't recall what year the trouble had begun or the name of the pills her drug-using daughter had been given by a friend. To avoid finding yourself in a similar situation, here is the information you should have on hand for an interview:

- The reasons you think your child has a problem. Be specific. What have you found, seen, or suspected?
- Family history in terms of the use of chemicals. Don't forget to include grandparents.
- History of behavioral and/or school-related problems.
- Current family stresses.
- Any previous attempts to secure treatment or alter the drug-use pattern. When? How? Where? How successful was it?

If both parents are to be present, make sure you and your spouse agree on the basic facts. This is not to say that parents will see the situation identically. On the contrary, they are more likely to have differing pictures. Disagreements during the interview can help the counselor see what is going on. However, prolonged squabbling over factual matters can be a time-waster.

If you are the only parent who believes there is a problem or are a single parent, stick to your convictions. Support and validation for your viewpoint from professionals or other parents will make it easier for you.

PROPELLING YOUR CHILD INTO ASSESSMENT AND TREATMENT

A few adolescents and young adults ask for help themselves because they feel so sick, guilty, or frightened that they don't know where to run. An Illinois high school student on cocaine and alcohol went to his school counselor and said, "I think I'm going crazy. Help me." But it is much more common to have parents propel their child into treatment while that child is still trying to con everyone into thinking there's nothing wrong. Some kids do not give in until you are at your wit's end.

The experts disagree about the best way to get your child to an assessment interview or into treatment. Some say, "She has to come willingly"; others say, "Use every trick you can think of if that's the only way." Here is a checklist of alternatives for you to consider for your own child:

1. Give him an ultimatum that he must go for help or be confined to home. One father told his son he couldn't go out the door until he went with him first to the local counseling center. The boy was petulant and angry, but he knew the only way out of the house was to go with his father. If you use this method, be sure you not only mean what you say, but are able to carry it out.
2. Withdraw any and all financial support—allowances, chores that are rewarded with cash, cash presents, etc. (The danger here is that your child may start dealing in drugs to get money.)
3. Impose strict sanctions. When asked what she would do if her child flatly refused help, Carol Burnett (whose daughter had a drug problem) said, "Then we'll make it

as rough as possible at home. We'll take away any belongings of value. We will ensure that they only go out to attend school and we will alert the school to the problem. If they get busted, we'll let them spend a night in jail. If they run away, we will report them to the police. If they're old enough to support themselves and insist on using drugs, our home will be closed to them. In short, we will only support a desire for help, not dope."

4. Get help for yourself so you can act more forcefully. A counselor says, "Many of the parents we see practice 'crossed-finger parenting.' They try something and hope it will work. We give them back their parenting power and show them how they can get their child to come in." Formal intervention, in which a counselor, the family, and friends meet with the drug abuser and present him or her with objective evidence of the harm the dependency is causing, is less common for teenagers. However, it can be very successful with young adults and is described in detail in Vernon Johnson's book *Intervention: How to Help Someone Who Doesn't Want Help.*

Sometimes parents have to use desperate measures. A mother tricked her child into joining a treatment program by telling him they were going to look for a secondhand television set. Once inside the unmarked building, he was whisked back to an interview room. A father captured his daughter and drove her to the hospital after "I tried everything. She had been drinking since she was fourteen and couldn't stop. At fifteen she was failing in school, not coming home nights. A school counselor told me about an inpatient program. I talked to them and we decided that was where she belonged. My son and I went to get her at school without telling her, and found her already outside, cutting classes. My son raced her down an alley, caught her, and forced her into the car. She's now been sober for three months."

Although these drastic, controversial approaches are not for everyone, they should be considered if you are stuck. You may have to act while your child is still reluctant, and the time when he is finally motivated to change may not come until treatment has been going on for some time. When a child is using drugs or alcohol he cannot make clear decisions in his own best interest.

THE ASSESSMENT INTERVIEW AND AFTERWARD

Once you have arranged for an assessment interview and you and your child have been seen (this may take several visits lasting two hours or more), you should know:

- The results of psychological tests (if they have been administered). "It's like doing an X ray to see what is wrong underneath," says the head of a storefront counseling center. "Only then can you start treatment."
- Whether your child is physically or psychologically drug-dependent. This will determine if she needs detoxification, which has to be done under close medical supervision.
- The kind of therapy recommended—outpatient, inpatient, or therapeutic community. As a general rule, the least restrictive environment (outpatient, for example) is the best way to start unless your child is clearly unmanageable at home.

- The names of counselors or facilities where drug treatment is provided in or near your community if outpatient help is recommended.
- The names and complete descriptions of places that are realistic and appropriate for your child and your family if inpatient treatment is recommended. Don't be misled by flashy brochures or extravagant claims of success.
- How your family will be involved in the treatment process. Will there be weekly sessions? An intensive "family week" program for parents?

After you have received recommendations from a counselor, you may still want a second opinion, particularly if you and your spouse disagree about what has been said.

TREATMENT CHOICES

Basically, adolescent drug abusers are treated in three different types of settings: drug-free outpatient; short-term inpatient; and therapeutic community. (For the small proportion of opiate abusers, there is also methadone maintenance—the use of a drug to block the craving for heroin, provided in an outpatient clinic. Some critics see this treatment as substituting one drug for another, but professionals generally consider it a valuable tool.) Most of these programs require that the participants also attend a support group based on the twelve steps of Alcoholics Anonymous.

When faced with several treatment options, paying attention to these factors will help you make an intelligent decision:

- Your child's age and maturity.
- Whether he or she suffers from depression or some other psychiatric disorder in addition to drug abuse. In professional parlance, this is called a "dual diagnosis" and may require treatment in a psychiatric hospital.
- Whether the treatment that is recommended is available in your area and is affordable.
- Whether insurance covers all or part of the costs. In this day of managed care, outpatient treatment, which is least expensive, may be the most realistic alternative. Some managed care programs require that a child first go through outpatient care unsuccessfully before moving to an inpatient setting. Often, inpatient care lasts just two days for stabilization and detoxification. Most insurance policies do not cover long-term residential care. Within the last five years, the emphasis on brief treatment and outpatient programs has played a part in forcing the closing of almost half the inpatient treatment centers in this country.
- Whether your child can stay drug-free at home and resist destructive peer pressure.

The most expensive help is not necessarily the best, and even with professional guidance you will want to do some comparison shopping.

Above all, you must be honest about your child. If your son is a long-haired streetwise kid, he may get along poorly with a business-suited psychotherapist and may do best with a storefront streetworker. On the other hand, sometimes a tough kid will need the structure of a formal office setting. If your child is the serious intellectual type, he may need an approach that emphasizes learning how to think about what is happening and why. This is called "cognitive therapy." A child who has long-standing psychological problems needs a setting that can deal with more than just the drug usage. A user who has disturbed his body chemistry with illicit substances needs an inpatient medical facility. A child who is what a counselor called a "brat" (irresponsible, uncontrollable, impulsive) will probably do best in a therapeutic community that provides a rigid structure and education on how to relate to others. It's important that you look as clearly as possible at the kind of child you have rather than the kind of child you wish you had, and fit the child to the treatment.

One mother whose son has abused "every drug but alcohol" visited a treatment center that required patients to live behind locked doors. "It looked seedy and dirty and I knew it wasn't for us," she says. She found another place in her own city that provided all-day care but let her son come home at night. Another parent, desperate to find a place her angry, rebellious son would accept, chose a facility from a brochure. "I thought he'd like it because he likes sunshine, and there were palm trees and beautiful grounds," she says. It was thousands of miles from home, and her son ran away the first month he was there.

DRUG-FREE OUTPATIENT PROGRAMS

Crisis intervention centers are often community-based storefront facilities staffed mainly by nonprofessionals who have themselves been drug abusers. They are not likely to fall for the youngster who says, "I experimented just that one time," or "I was keeping the stuff for a friend." The centers provide emergency help, short-term treatment, and evaluation and referral. Says George Doering, Jr., director of the Ramapo Counseling Center in Spring Valley, New York, "Sometimes it's just a question of giving a kid the opportunity to grow up with some support. For a lot of kids, four to six months of treatment are fine." These centers can also be used as a transition into more intensive care or for aftercare once a child has returned from inpatient treatment.

Psychotherapy and counseling are usually provided in a clinic or mental health center or by a private practitioner. The therapist is usually a psychiatrist, psychologist, social worker, credentialed alcoholism counselor, drug abuse counselor, or pastoral counselor. Talking about personal problems on a one-to-one basis is the crux of this treatment method, which may also offer other services such as peer groups and family therapy.

Finding the right counselor is vital. To assess one, you should know:

- What kind of formal training the counselor has; how much and what kind of experience he or she has had with chemically dependent people. (If the therapist has the basic tools and is honest and caring, the professional label is not of great importance.)
- Whether this person insists on no drug or alcohol use during treatment. (There is general agreement that abstinence is essential, but no agreement on giving up cigarettes simultaneously.)
- What knowledge the counselor has of self-help programs.
- How he or she views adolescent drug use. Authorities

agree that anything beyond fleeting experimentation
should be taken seriously.

- If you are comfortable with this person and if you think
your child will be.
- If you can ask questions without feeling that you are an
overanxious parent.
- Whether you will have regular meetings with your
child's therapist or counselor to discuss what progress is
being made, how he or she sees your child's problem, and
what the long-term treatment plans and prognosis are.
You have a right to know what you're paying for—not
the details, but the general outline.

If the first person you interview doesn't seem right, keep
trying.

Sometimes finding the right person is as much a matter
of luck as of sophisticated choice-making. When one
mother finally cajoled her son into accompanying her to a
psychologist's office, the man pulled a form from his top
drawer and, looking down at the page, asked, "Birth
weight?" Mother and son knew immediately they were in
the wrong place. The next person they saw was a youth ad-
vocate whose storefront office was part of a community out-
reach program. The worker was not much older than his
client, had been through a drug treatment program, and
was clearly familiar with this kind of kid.

All-day treatment centers and alternative day schools op-
erate from early morning to evening and provide a highly
structured environment that includes school, chores, peer
counseling, and individual counseling. The youngsters are
taken out of their usual daily environment and go home
only to sleep. The staff is made up largely of recovering al-

cohol and drug abusers, who are often supervised by mental health professionals. Family participation is an important part of the program, and those who graduate from day treatment usually attend aftercare programs there so that they aren't abruptly thrown back into the outside world. Youngsters are often in treatment for a year or more.

After-school programs are designed to catch the drug use before it gets too bad. These use confrontational techniques, peer pressure, family participation, and other techniques to help a child stay in his or her regular school setting.

INPATIENT PROGRAMS

Despite differing orientations and theoretical backgrounds, most treatment programs have similar goals:

- To help your child live a drug-free life. The general attitude, says Dr. David Smith of the Haight-Ashbury Free Clinic, is that "once a person has crossed the boundary into uncontrollable use, she/he may never return to controlled use. It's as if one catches the disease for which abstinence is the cure."
- To help your child grow into a different person, with a better set of values and a new self-image. (Sometimes more extensive therapy is necessary to achieve this goal once the drug is out of the picture.)
- To help the family function more effectively.

Inpatient programs traditionally have been twenty-one to twenty-eight days long, based on the adult model developed for the treatment of alcohol abuse. Although some insurance plans cover this type of treatment program, most managed care plans do not. An average stay today is usually two weeks. Treatment may be in a hospital (psychiatric or general) or a separate facility, and the doors may be locked or unlocked. They usually include detoxification (medically supervised withdrawal from the drug), if this is necessary. They are professionally staffed and include individual and group counseling and education about drug and alcohol abuse as well as the reestablishment of general good health with facilities for exercise and physical fitness. A child who needs this kind of setting is not necessarily sicker than one who doesn't—he may just have different requirements. Youngsters with underlying psychiatric disorders may need hospital treatment so that both the depression, for example, and drug abuse can be addressed. Unfortunately, treatment time is often based on length of insurance coverage. Most facilities either provide continuing groups for their "graduates" or refer them to easily accessible outpatient care. Some go on to halfway houses where recovering youngsters live in a supervised setting until they are ready to return home.

Therapeutic communities provide long-term (eighteen months to two years) residential treatment using "boot camp" confrontational techniques and positive peer pressure. Some of the earlier harsh methods have been toned down and made more supportive, but staffing is still largely by recovering addicts who know what the story is and don't fall for rationalizations. Mutual self-help, public criticism, and self-criticism characterize the approach. Time is tightly structured, and youngsters learn by living that it is possible to get through a drug-free day. The program, in essence, gives them a second chance at childhood, carefully guided and with strict but supportive substitute parents. Some well-established therapeutic communities are Daytop Village and Phoenix House, which have treatment centers in New York, California, and Texas. When you are investigating an inpatient facility of whatever type, you should:

- Be nosy. Ask questions at the facility and in the community in which it operates. What do people say about it? What do they think of the youngsters who go there?
- Not sign anything unless you are absolutely sure you have found the right place.
- Consider carefully if you are asked to pay anything in advance. Most places will accept insurance for at least part of the cost. If you are in a managed care program, check for what your plan does or does not cover.
- Be wary if the common prohibition against parent-child phone calls, letters, and private meetings goes on for more than the first one or two months. Isolation from the family is often called for in the early phase of treatment, but reintegration into the family is usually one of the goals of the later phases.

HELP FOR FAMILIES

When asked, "What works as far as treatment is concerned?" counselors say, "The intense involvement of the parents." When your child enters treatment, it will not be, as one counselor said, "like sending him to the cleaners and expecting him to come back pressed." You and the rest of the family will have to be part of the process. "The child's crisis with alcohol and drugs is a way for him to cry out for help for himself and the rest of the family," says an experienced therapist. "Paradoxically, it may also be an attempt to remove the focus from his parents if they are having problems and keep them together as they rally around him and his troubles."

Families have a wide range of choices. They may participate in a family week at an inpatient facility; they may be part of a parents' group in an inpatient or a day program; they may have joint therapy sessions with other families along with their addicted youngsters; or they may see a counselor to help them understand what is happening and how they can cope.

Why should you get involved? The father of a drug abuser who was being treated as an outpatient put it this way: "I didn't want to go to the parents' group, but it was nice to know we weren't the only people in the world who were desperate. Before we went, I was ashamed. I felt I had failed. The group gave us structure and strength. We learned that we had to get the idea across that we are his parents, that we care, and that he's still our child."

If you join a parents' group, you may feel awkward at first. But people in the group will stop being strangers once they begin to talk openly about concerns that you share. You might hear someone else say, "Well, I'm here because I just don't know what else to do." Soon you will feel freer about telling your story, and everyone will be looking for solutions to problems with children, yours as well as theirs.

Sometimes programs have family therapy available, bringing together not only parents but all the available children in the family. In a variation on this method called "multiple family therapy," several families meet on a regular basis. Seeing how another family operates can lead to a surprised recognition of the rough spots in your own family and to learning ways in which you might act to protect your other children. The father of a nineteen-year-old alcoholic daughter said at the end of one such session: "I didn't know what I sounded like until I heard John yell at his daughter. It was like seeing a videotape of how our family works. Before this, I didn't know anything was wrong— with her or with us. Boy, have things changed!"

SELF-HELP THERAPIES

In most treatment programs, attendance for the youngster at self-help meetings (based on the Alcoholics Anonymous twelve-step program) begins during treatment and continues afterward. Sometimes a child is able to leave alcohol and/or other drugs behind just by using the time-honored self-help approach, but most of the time it requires a total treatment plan.

Special Alcoholics Anonymous (AA) groups for teenage drinkers have sprung up all over the country. The meetings are free, and you can find out when and where they are held by calling Alcoholics Anonymous, listed in your local phone book. Since so many teenagers abuse more than one drug, there will be people there who can support your child's efforts to stay away from any drug.

Because of the explosive growth of drug abuse over the past few years, Narcotics Anonymous (NA) and Nar-Anon have gained members. Their approach is modeled on the twelve steps of Alcoholics Anonymous.

What are the advantages of NA over AA? Addicts answer that they seek fellowship with other addicts. Many consider addiction to alcohol different because alcohol is not an illegal drug for adults. The addicted NA members use heroin, cocaine, or prescription drugs as well as marijuana. In some areas, there are specialized meetings, such as Cocaine Anonymous. Your child will be welcome wherever he feels he belongs.

OBSTACLES TO RECOVERY

Once your child has started to get help, you may breathe a sigh of relief. But the battle is not over. There are still obstacles ahead, both during treatment and when your child comes home. Here are some of them:

DROPOUT RATE

Youngsters who are going to drop out of programs are most likely to do so during the first ninety days. During that critical time, you have to do everything you can to encourage and even push your child to stick with it. The study of adolescent drug use prepared by the Rand Corporation, a California think tank, reported as a "disturbing characteristic of all treatment programs [that] more than half of all admissions terminate prematurely, either by dropping out or by being dismissed by the treatment facility for rule violations." Youngsters who stay through the whole course of treatment, whether inpatient or outpatient, short-term or long-term, are most likely to recover. But even if your child does drop out, don't be discouraged. There's always another chance.

PLEAS

One mother says the hardest thing she ever did was to walk away when her son pleaded with her to "get me out of here." He was in a chemical dependency unit in a hospital and wept as each visit was ending. Of course, you can't ignore signs that this is not the right place for your child, but you have to guard against giving in because you feel guilty for having put your child in other people's hands.

RELAPSES

It is impossible to avoid the one big worry—will your daughter or son begin using drugs or alcohol again? Although you may be overly watchful for signs during and after treatment, you have to accept the reality that you cannot control another human being—even your own child.

In fact, relapses are an expected part of the process. A boy who had attended an all-day program for a little over a year started smoking marijuana again while he was at his parents' vacation house. Word got back to his counselor (his friends had adopted a new code: "snitching" is good and may save a life), and his parents were told to bring him in. He was confronted by his group while his parents were told to "take a walk." "He took a step backward," his mother says, "but just a step. Nobody promised us it would be quick and easy." He was threatened with confinement in a live-in facility, but to everyone's relief, this wasn't necessary and he went on to become drug-free.

HOMECOMING

Treatment is not finished when your child returns home full-time. For many, this is the start of a difficult phase of rehabilitation. In fact, what goes on now will often make the difference.

You may be expecting a resurgence of domestic turmoil. Some family members may feel shy or embarrassed or just plain curious. Even if you are apprehensive, you have to greet the "new" family member with understanding so he or she will feel truly at home. Being shunned or looked upon as a curiosity may create the temptation to slide back into old ways. New ways, developed during treatment, may be disturbing, too. Your child may be better, but he will not be the same. He may be more independent, more outspoken, or he may surprise you and be more compliant.

You may find that your child does not accept the goals you had once set, and this will be painful. But having come out of a fog, he may now know himself better and have more realistic expectations for himself.

Your child will also make new friends, and they may not be the friends you would pick. They, too, may be "graduates" of whatever program he participated in. Sometimes it feels uncomfortable when a child chooses to confide in a friend rather than in a family member, but unfortunately, you will have no choice. This is normal adolescent behavior.

As to the whole upsetting period of drug use, families react in different ways. Once the terrible time has been lived through, some families say, "We never talk about that anymore." Some youngsters choose to keep the experience to themselves and will share it only with a counselor or friend. Yet some recovering kids love to talk about their troubles over and over again. Tolerate it. Listen. It will mean a lot to your child to know that you care and are interested, and it will bring family members closer together.

Whatever the attitude, one way you can be helpful is to make sure your child knows that the family plans to continue therapy and expects him or her to do the same. Here are some other practical suggestions for any parent who is welcoming home a newly abstinent, drug-free member of the family:

- Rid your household of liquor. Don't forget the beer in the refrigerator. Alcohol consumption makes it more likely that drug use—of whatever kind—will start again.
- Don't leave money on dresser tops or anyplace where it can be picked up.
- Keep your car keys in your pocket. You should have control over who uses them and when.
- Be alert when your youngster has visitors.
- Be awake when your child comes home at night.
- Be absolutely clear about what is and what is not permitted in your home (parties, music, drinks, smoking, etc.).
- If you've made a family contract, go over it and be sure it is still up-to-date and understood (see p. 112).

BACK TO SCHOOL

One youngster said, "It's not as hard to go home as it is to go back to school." He's right, because in school, your child will once again be with the kids with whom he did drugs. The child has learned to say no, but the temptation will be there, and a lot of it may come from students who will try to lure him back into the drug scene or make fun of him for having been caught or for going "straight." On the other hand, there will be new friends who will respect him for having turned around and will not try to undermine his commitment.

You can try to hook him up with a counselor or psychologist in school or a student assistance program. Some high schools have special classes or sections for students who have been rehabilitated to provide a buffer between them and those who are still using. Deerfield High School in Illinois assigns each returning youngster to a student who has been back in school for a while and can act as a guide. A "Reaching Out Room" in which these students can eat lunch and build new friendships with other recovering kids is also part of the program. This room is staffed all day, so there is always someone to talk to when the going gets rough.

DEFINITIONS OF SUCCESS

Once their children have recovered, parents report:

"I don't feel I have to worry about him anymore."

"It's great to have my own child back again."

"She's better than she's ever been."

"It was like a death and now he has a second chance."

"As much as my son changed, I've changed more."

These parents were all optimistic, yet the scorecard of achievement for treatment programs is mixed. Some studies that have looked at results show that the longer treatment lasts, the better the chance of success. There is also the grim reality, according to Dr. Ingrid Lantner, a pioneer in the field who looked at the studies as well as her own cases, that "no matter what kind of treatment is given, the success rate is about 50 percent." It's important to understand, though, that statistics have nothing to do with individuals, and your child has as good a chance of being among those who recover as among those who don't. Hope is a powerful medicine that should not be discounted.

What seems like success to one parent may seem like a compromise to another. Sometimes you have to settle for less than the dream. Looking back after seven years, one mother in a parents' group said, "I used to think that if my kid stopped, then life would go on as if nothing had happened. But my definition of success has changed. I'm not going to have a son who graduates from college. If I'm very lucky, I'll have a son who won't ever be what he might have been, but he'll be healthy." She adds, "There was a long period of reconciliation to get here—it's really hard to give up your dreams for your child even if they're not the child's dream."

Sometimes the goal of a drug-free life is not achieved, yet the youngster is able to live a better life. The daughter of divorced parents was so alienated in the family that she ate alone in her room and had her own Christmas tree there. She hardly spoke to her mother and chose to spend most of her time with her father. She was on LSD, Quaaludes, and marijuana when she saw a therapist because she couldn't recover from a "bad trip." She was fifteen years old. After outpatient treatment, she finished high school, got into college, then dropped out. She is now nineteen, working, and, says her therapist, "comparatively drug-free. She uses a little pot."

The same therapist encouraged a girl who had been using marijuana as medication for depression to "use me instead of pot." Here, too, treatment results were mixed but encouraging. The sixteen-year-old, who asked for treatment herself, went from being "the most depressed child the school had ever seen" and someone who associated with a delinquent gang to someone who traveled with an "artsy" crowd. With the help of tutoring, her grades went up and her self-concept shifted from "I'm stupid and delinquent" to "I'm creative and different." Her drug use dropped dramatically. The therapist suggested that her parents think of her as "an eccentric relative," and everyone is now comfortable with her new image. As she matures, chances are much better than they might have been that she will go on to be completely drug-free.

WHAT IF...

How will you feel when you have seen a counselor, spent thousands of dollars and hundreds of sleepless nights, had countless arguments with your husband or wife and friends, had several encounters with law enforcement agencies, and carefully selected what you thought was best—and nothing has worked? Your kid is worse than ever. He is staying out late, not showing up at school, lying, stealing, threatening to run away, and making life miserable for everyone. The treatment has not helped. This does happen, and we all have to face the reality that for some drug addicts and alcoholics there may be hope, but very little else. Until things reach some kind of equilibrium, you will have to do whatever is necessary to go on with your own life while keeping the door open for your child.

On the other hand, many cases that looked hopeless have finally yielded to treatment. The mother of such a boy says, "Never say never," and gives this advice to other parents:

- Don't give up hope. Even small signs can be a cause for optimism. If your child is beginning to ask why or how he got into the predicament he's in; if he's home more; if his brothers and sisters are talking to him more; if he gets to school more regularly, you can feel encouraged. Keep looking for the right help. If one kind doesn't work, another might.
- Make sure everyone is involved. It's a family problem. Don't overlook the other children, who may be as frightened and perplexed as you are.
- Listen to the prescription. Do what is suggested. You may have to put your own life on "hold" for a while.

One family put its life aside with results that can bring hope to others. "We had a terrorist living in our home. Now that he is off drugs, our life has changed. We have a healthy son and a much healthier family life." Dennis had conned everyone during high school, using pot and pills and drinking heavily. When he finally went into a strict treatment program for a year and a half, his battered family had a chance to catch its breath and begin to feel that there was hope for the future. The whole family was involved in treatment every weekend, and now that he is drug-free, home, and working, they go to Al-Anon regularly and he goes to AA and Nar-Anon.

In a Christmas letter to their friends, Dennis's relieved parents wrote:

> You may have wondered why you haven't heard from us during the past two years . . . why no one answered the phone; why we were rarely seen in town; why we had, in a way, disappeared. Well, we haven't dropped off the edge of the planet, but we've been coping with a serious family illness.
>
> To make a very long and arduous story short, we found that our son, Dennis, whom many of you have known for years, had become chemically dependent. We would have lost him if it had not been for the availability of a vigorous treatment program. . . .
>
> Our energy to give to friends and social life dwindled to zero, but we had no choice if Dennis was to regain his health and our family was to revive. These years have been painful but worth every bit of what we've put into them. Dennis is recovering . . . and so are we. Our love to you. Merry Christmas . . . it is a Happy New Year.

PART 3

Information for Parents

Drug Dictionary

NOTE: Much of the material in the Drug Dictionary can be found in *Research Issues 26—Guide to Drug Abuse Research Terminology*, published by the National Institute of Drug Abuse under the U.S. Department of Health and Human Services.

We also want to thank Dr. Stephen J. Donovan, assistant professor of clinical psychiatry, College of Physicians and Surgeons, Columbia University, for his invaluable contribution in reviewing this material.

Addiction   is an overpowering, recurrent, excessive need for a substance that is used in spite of the costs to one's physical, social, emotional, or economic well-being. Symptoms are: (1) a compulsion to use mood-altering drugs; (2) a loss of control over the use of those drugs; and (3) continual use despite adverse consequences.

AIDS   (Acquired Immunodeficiency Syndrome) causes the body to lose its natural defenses against disease, making it vulnerable to many illnesses which it is then unable to fight off. There is no known cure for AIDS, but it can be treated to prolong life.

One way AIDS is spread from one person to another is by using shared needles to inject drugs. Someone who doesn't inject drugs can acquire the virus from a sexual partner who is an infected intravenous drug user. AIDS can also be spread by infected blood that gets into an open wound.

There is no evidence that AIDS is spread by any other nonsexual physical contact. For example, you cannot contract the virus from exposure to toilet seats, cigarette butts, showers, handshakes, dishes, food, doorknobs, linens, clothing, sneezing, coughing, spitting, or from being around a person with AIDS. Symptoms of AIDS include fatigue, dizziness, night sweats, unexplained weight loss, coughing, bleeding, shortness of breath, and bruises. Parents should remember that these symptoms are seen in many other illnesses, so you should not panic or jump to any kind of conclusion. If you are concerned, consult your physician or call the AIDS HOTLINE (1-800-342-2437).

Alcohol is a central nervous system (CNS) depressant found in wine, beer, and hard liquor. It is easily obtainable, but is an illicit drug for people under age twenty-one. When ingested, it is absorbed quickly into the bloodstream and then goes to the brain. Packages are required by law to display a warning against use by pregnant women, since a mother's drinking can harm the fetus. Its effects are different for different people, but for most it produces a relaxed feeling of well-being at first. Then it leads to dizziness, scrambled thoughts, slurred speech, and lack of coordination—what is commonly known as drunkenness and intoxication.

These effects depend upon how fast the beverage is ingested, the weight of the drinker, how much food is in the stomach when the drinking takes place, and how accustomed the drinker is to drinking.

Alcohol is broken down (metabolized) by the body at the rate of about half an ounce of pure alcohol (roughly the amount in one highball, one can of beer, or one glass of wine) per hour. Contrary to common myths, this process cannot be speeded up by taking showers, drinking coffee, or exercising. Only time will allow the body to rid itself of the drug.

Alcohol is dangerous because it acts as a temporary mood elevator. While "high," many people increase their risk-taking behavior. High doses, rapidly ingested, can lead to irregular heartbeats, asphyxiation, and death by overdose. Because alcohol is so rapidly absorbed, emergency treatment must be fast. When combined with other depressant drugs, alcohol is particularly dangerous because of the cumulative depressant effect. When used in conjunction with other drugs, even a small dose can be lethal.

When alcohol is used excessively and regularly, over time, alcoholism, an illness, develops. The user becomes physiologically addicted and develops some tolerance. He has withdrawal symptoms (shakes, sweats, and more) when the drinking stops.

Amphetamines are synthetically produced central nervous system stimulants. Their trade names include Dexedrine, Adderal, and DextroStat. They are also known as speed, uppers, crank, pep pills, meth, or bennies. They are generally taken in tablet form, but sometimes are injected or snorted. Effects include increased heart and breathing rates, wakefulness, restlessness, feelings of elation, talkativeness, and volatile behavior. When these drugs are used regularly or excessively, they lead to confusion, paranoia, sleeplessness, belligerence, and hallucinations. Pupils become dilated, and there is increased perspiration and loss of appetite. Effects start in about thirty minutes and last from four to fourteen hours. All amphetamine-like drugs have a high potential for psychological dependence and limited, low-grade physical dependence. In chronic use, tolerance occurs.

Symptoms of withdrawal include depression, sleepiness, paranoia, nightmares, hunger, and cramps. Sometimes the user looks as if he were having an asthma attack. Withdrawal is treated with counseling and sedative drugs that should be taken only under a physician's care.

Young people use amphetamines to lose weight, to keep awake before exams, and to encourage a feeling of fearlessness comparable to the effect of the body's own adrenaline.

Anabolic Steroids are closely related to the male hormone, testosterone. They can be injected or taken orally. Although prohibited by all amateur and professional sports organizations, they are taken by almost 500,000 teen athletes to build muscles and improve strength. They are also used by young men who want to achieve a "macho" image. The drugs are available on the black market or through health professionals. Continued use of steroids can cause effects ranging from acne and aching joints to liver damage and cancers. Physical symptoms include weight and muscle gain, purple or red spots on the body, and a persistent unpleasant breath odor. Regular users quickly become psychologically dependent and may be subject to wide mood swings, aggressive behavior, and even psychosis. Adolescents who use steroids have been found to be more likely to use other illicit drugs.

Barbiturates   are sedative hypnotic drugs that depress the central nervous system. They are used as sleeping pills and in anesthesia to produce rapid unconsciousness. Their trade names include Seconal, Nembutal, secobarbital, and pentobarbital. They are also known as barbs, downers, reds, yellow jackets, purple hearts, blues, goof balls, or rainbows.

Barbiturates are prepared as capsules, tablets, liquids, or suppositories. Their effects of sleepy, drowsy feelings last from four to six hours, and in some cases up to twelve hours. In small doses, the user becomes uncoordinated and unaware of physical surroundings and may even trip or walk into objects. Such doses reduce anxiety and produce a mild euphoria and muscular relaxation. Users feel groggy as the effects wear off. Larger doses induce sleep, but can also produce effects similar to drunkenness in addition to depression, anxiety, and unpredictability. High doses are dangerous and can lead to depression of the respiratory control center of the brain, resulting in shallow breathing, unconsciousness, and ultimately death. Long-term use of these drugs results in tolerance and addiction. Sudden withdrawal is dangerous and should be undertaken only with medical supervision.

Use of barbiturates with other CNS depressants, such as alcohol, is common and greatly increases the user's chances of overdosing. Barbiturates are more often involved in suicides and accidental drug poisoning than are other sedative hypnotics. Users are often not aware of the "additive" or "potentiation" effects when two or more depressants are used concurrently. In cases of overdosing, the user should be given immediate medical attention.

Benzodiazepines are sedative hypnotics. Benzodiazepines are known as anti-anxiety agents or minor tranquilizers. Trade names include Librium, Valium, Tranxene, Serax, and Ativan. These come in tablet or capsule form, and since they are commonly found in household medicine cabinets, they should be guarded or counted. There is little difference in their pharmacological effects except duration of action.

Effects include calmness, sedation, euphoria, loss of coordination, sleepiness, and general lethargy. Large doses can cause delirium, nightmares, and delusions. Withdrawal symptoms, like those of barbiturates, include restlessness, cramps, shaking, weakness, and insomnia. Benzodiazepines are all mildy addictive.

Caffeine   is a central nervous system stimulant. It is found in coffee, tea, cola drinks, chocolate, cocoa, certain prescription medications, and such over-the-counter stay-awake pills as No-Doz and Vivarin. It is a white, crystalline substance that affects the brain and is a natural part of certain plants. Effects vary widely from person to person. It constricts blood vessels and acts as a mild stimulant fifteen to thirty minutes after ingestion. Moderate doses are used to combat drowsiness. High doses cause insomnia, shakiness, and feelings of generalized tension. In some, caffeine can produce irregular heart rhythms and/or high blood pressure. Toxic overdoses are rare, but caffeine-caused convulsions and death from respiratory failure have been reported. Regular coffee drinkers can become addicted and may develop tolerance and feel jittery or develop a headache when they are deprived of the drug. Contrary to popular belief, caffeine does not significantly counter alcohol intoxication.

Central Nervous System (CNS)   refers to the brain and spinal cord, which are the primary systems affected by psychoactive drugs. The initials CNS are often used when referring to the two major classes of psychoactive drugs—CNS depressants and CNS stimulants.

Cocaine   is a central nervous system stimulant. It is also known as flake or snow because it looks like a crystalline white powder. Like sugar, it is odorless, but it has a bitter taste. It is nearly always diluted with sugar and/or local anesthetics such as procaine, which make it more palatable and cheaper per gram. Cocaine is commonly sniffed or "snorted" through a straw or a rolled-up dollar bill. It is soluble in water and can therefore be injected. Effects include dilated pupils, sweating, runny nose, dry mouth, increased heart rate, and elevated blood pressure. The user feels little pain or fatigue. These effects begin within a few minutes, peak within ten minutes, and wear off within half an hour. In low doses, cocaine produces a short-lived intense exhilaration, a sense of well-being, alertness, and energy, and a depressed appetite. In high doses, it produces hallucinations, imaginary persecutions, and paranoia. When used regularly, it has serious consequences, including depression, suicidal tendencies, lack of energy or drive, and a feeling of being washed out. Cocaine produces both dependence and withdrawal symptoms. The drive to reexperience the euphoria is often overwhelming, and it is possible to take a lethal dose. Even one dose can be fatal. Cocaine abuse is often associated with the use of a sedative to take the edge off the high.

Parents should remember that cocaine metabolites are excreted in the urine and detection is possible for two to four days after use.

Codeine is a narcotic/analgesic present in the opiate poppy plant along with morphine. It is a chemical closely related to morphine, but is much less potent. Medically, it is used as a painkiller and to prevent coughing. It can produce nausea and constipation and low-grade withdrawal effects.

Propoxyphene hydrochloride (the main active ingredient in Darvon) has similar effects.

Crack is cocaine in smokable (free-base) form. It is "cooked" by the dealer and made into crack.

Crack is sold in small gray or beige chunks, chips, or shavings. These are packaged in small, varicolored capsules or glass tubes or in heat-sealed envelopes. The user pulverizes the chunks, which are then smoked on a tobacco or marijuana cigarette or through a special pipe. The rapid onset of action makes the effects more intense than cocaine taken in other forms. There is a new form of crack in pill form that can be swallowed, but oral doses are not very effective. It is said that once crack is used two or three times, it is almost impossible to stop. The user feels that it is as necessary for life as food, water, or air. Yet crack users have recovered.

Some of the effects of crack are violence, irrational behavior, insomnia, memory problems, depression, fatigue, and suicide attempts. Some users have seizures, heart attacks, strokes, and cessation of breathing. Crack users give up on all aspects of personal life. Many become addicted to CNS depressants, including alcohol, as they try to ameliorate the effects of coming off the cocaine-produced high.

Cross-tolerance is a condition in which decreased response to one drug because of chronic use results in decreased response to other drugs in the same class.

Dalmane is a benzodiazepine. It is relatively safe compared to barbiturates because the lethal dose is much larger than the effective dose. Dalmane is frequently prescribed by physicians for sleep. It is commonly found in household medicine chests and therefore should be carefully guarded.

Demerol is a narcotic/analgesic. It is an analgesic (anti-pain) drug similar in action to morphine and is often prescribed by physicians for severe pain. Since it is found in many household medicine chests, it should be guarded. It is psychologically and physically addictive.

Dependence can be physical, psychological, or both. Physical dependence is a state of physiological adaptation to the presence of a drug in the body. Following the development of tolerance and dependence, a characteristic withdrawal syndrome is observed after discontinuation of the drug. Dependence is a synonym for addiction.

Psychological dependence is a broad term generally referring to a craving for or compulsion to continue the use of a drug that gives satisfaction or a feeling of well-being. Psychological dependence may vary in intensity from a mild preference to a strong craving or compulsion to use the drug.

Depressants (CNS) can be divided into four major categories: alcohol, opiates, sedative/hypnotics, and volatile inhalants. All affect the CNS similarly in a progression—depending on dosage—from reduction of anxiety to sedation, hypnosis (sleep), anesthesia, coma, and even death. The immediate effects include sedation and a decrease in bodily activity, not to be confused with the psychological state of depression. These drugs can, in fact, act as mood-elevators by lowering inhibitions. Most important, they have an additive effect, so that when they are used together, they compound the effects of each other and greatly increase the risk of death. Alcohol is the most commonly used depressant and should never be taken in combination with other depressant drugs.

Designer Drugs   are specially crafted imitations of various drugs "designed" to escape legal identification as illicit and are therefore outside or above the law. In other words, underground chemists fashion their own concoctions, often in their own kitchens, and the user rarely knows what he is getting. The drugs are usually hallucinogens such as these:

- **DMT**   (dimethyltryptamine) is similar to psilocin (psilocybin), and its effects are similar to LSD. DMT effects begin almost immediately and last less than an hour.
- **MDA**   (methylene dioxyamphetamine) and **MDMA** (methylene diosymethamphetamine) are hallucinogens related synthetically to amphetamines and in action to adrenaline. MDMA is also known as "Ecstasy," and is associated particularly with "raves," all-night dance parties frequented by teens and college students. MDA and MDMA are ingested orally and share some of the effects of LSD. In high doses they are associated with severe excitation, hallucinations, confusion, and

sometimes convulsions. Several deaths have been at-
tributed to these drugs.

- **Special K**   (ketamine hydrochloride) is a powerful
  hallucinogen also associated with "raves." Used as an
  animal tranquilizer by veterinarians, it is produced by
  heating the liquid drug until it becomes a powder. It
  is usually snorted, but can also be sprinkled on tobacco or marijuana and smoked.
- **TMA**   (trimethoxyamphetamine) is another hallucinogen, with effects similar to LSD and Special K.

DOM   (dimethoxymethamphetamine) is the street drug
STP. It is related chemically to amphetamines and
mescaline and is said to produce an LSD-like experience.
It is smoked, snorted, or injected. Its primary effect is a
relentless rush of energy that causes users to tremble.
Users report a long "comedown" period of two or three
days and thus prefer to use the shorter-acting LSD.

Withdrawal symptoms have not been documented for
designer drugs.

Drug   Any substance that chemically changes the function of living tissues. The changes may be psychological,
physical, or both. All drugs are potential poisons, and
therefore can be dangerous if taken by the wrong person,
in the wrong amounts, at the wrong time, or in the
wrong combinations.

Psychoactive drugs are natural or synthetic substances
that change mental processes by altering mood and behavior. They are also known as mind- or mood-altering
drugs.

Drug Abuse   is the irresponsible use of potentially hazardous chemical substances, legal or illegal. Generally, it

implies chemical use that results in changes in some aspect of a person's life.

Flashbacks   are recurrences of druglike effects months or even years after drug use has ended. They remind the user of the drug experience and are usually tremendously anxiety-provoking, although some people report them as pleasant. Flashbacks may represent permanent brain damage caused by the chemical taken. See also LSD.

Free Base.   See Crack.

Gateway Drugs   are tobacco, alcohol, and marijuana, so-called because they are most often used first before users go on to stronger drugs. Regular, heavy use may prime the brain to respond to other, more powerful substances.

Hallucinogens   include synthetics such as LSD, MDA, MDMA, PCP, Special K, STP, DOM, and DMT, and the naturally occurring mescaline (peyote) and mushrooms containing psilocybin or psilocin. These are "mind-changers," the psychedelic drugs. They all produce hallucinations, which are defined as the perception of sounds, odors, tactile sensations, or visual images that arise from within the person but cannot be substantiated by external reality.

In low doses, effects vary widely depending on the drug taken and the unique sensitivity of the user. They may produce exhilaration or depression and can lead to psychoses and suicidal or homicidal tendencies.

Other effects include dilated pupils, hilarity, emotional swings, suspicious or bizarre behavior, nausea, and increased blood pressure. Higher doses produce the same symptoms plus convulsions and respiratory distress. Tolerance develops at different rates for different drugs.

Withdrawal symptoms have been documented after chronic use of especially the amphetamine-related substances and include depression, sleepiness, and low energy levels.

Treatment of bad trips: Place user in an isolated environment, reduce sensory stimulation (i.e., draw blinds, turn off music, cut out sounds), and calmly "talk the person down" (especially with PCP psychosis).

Hashish is a strong form of marijuana containing a higher concentration of THC, the active ingredient also found in marijuana. (Hashish can contain up to 15 percent THC, whereas marijuana usually contains only 1 to 5 percent.) It is also known as hash. It comes in many different shapes, but is often sold in little rectangular brown or black tablets. They may be crumbly or hard. It is smoked in water pipes that regulate and cool the smoke or is sprinkled on marijuana or tobacco cigarettes. It has a heavy marijuana odor when burned.

Heroin (diacetylmorphine) is a narcotic/analgesic, a central nervous system depressant. A semi-synthetic derivative of morphine, it is also known as horse, junk, dope, or smack. It is a crystalline, odorless, bitter-tasting white powder that is soluble in water. Most users inject the drug, but recently its increased purity and potency have made it possible to snort it, smoke it, or swallow it in capsules to avoid the hazards of needles and possible exposure to AIDS while still getting an intense reaction. When it is injected frequently, "tracks" along veins, usually on the arm, are visible.

The effect of heroin is that of a painkiller that leads to general lethargy. When injected, it produces an intense, orgasmic "rush" followed by euphoria and feelings of peacefulness, warmth, and comfort. Pulse and respiration slow down.

Tolerance builds rapidly, especially to the sedative effects, and addiction can be established in one to three weeks. Users are rarely hungry or in pain—they therefore become malnourished and develop vascular problems from frequent heroin injections. Infections, including AIDS and hepatitis, can result from the use of unsterilized or shared needles.

Withdrawal is difficult. It is an ordeal of intense cramps, sweats, delirium, pain, fever, anxiety, headaches, and often life-threatening seizures. The process begins four to eight hours after drug cessation and lasts three or four days.

With repeated use a high tolerance deprives the chronic user of the rush, but he or she still experiences the feeling of well-being and will escalate the dosage to recapture the original feelings.

Inhalants or **Volatile Anesthetic Solvents** depress the central nervous system. These chemicals are very easily available and are found in more than one thousand household products, including cleaning fluid, gasoline, plastic cement, nail polish remover, computer cleaner, model cement, paint thinner, spray starch, and thousands of industrial solvents having toluene, benzene, or naphtha bases. Contents of spray cans or room deodorants and cleaning fluids contain some of these intoxicating dangerous solvents, too. They are inhaled, "huffed" through the mouth, or sniffed. In low doses their effects include intoxication, dizziness, a floating sensation, an intense feeling of well-being, and a breakdown of inhibitions.

Low doses leave the system in fifteen minutes to a few hours.

As doses increase, so does tolerance, and then judgment is impaired, and users may have accidents, fights, and other life-threatening incidents. Inhalants are all mildly dependence-producing, so that after withdrawal, users feel nausea, depression, insomnia, and loss of appetite.

"Sudden sniffing death" is related to heart failure when the user is involved with vigorous physical exercise after sniffing a volatile hydrocarbon (found in aerosol sprays). Suffocation can occur when a plastic bag is used to concentrate vapors.

Using inhalants while taking other drugs, particularly depressants, slows down the body's functions. Loss of consciousness, coma, or death may result.

Since organic solvents are found in every American household and are widely advertised, they can be used by children as young as five years old. Older youths sometimes encourage their younger friends to "try it" for fun. Parents will know inhalants are being used by their strong odor.

Legal Highs   are legal herbs, spices, plants, and chemicals with psychoactive properties. They include dozens of substances commonly found in the home, such as nutmeg, mace, catnip, and hops, and also garden broom, hydrangea, and heliotrope. They produce a broad range of effects, including hallucinations, stimulation, and sedation. Herbal ecstasy, a combination of various herbs, is sold in health food stores, drugstores, and music shops, and has been implicated in serious side effects and even death. These substances usually require an extraction process to bring out the active ingredients. Many are toxic at high doses or when ingested in an improper amount or form and are often accompanied by unpleasant side effects such as nausea.

Librium.   See Benzodiazepines.

Look-Alike drugs are fake substitutes for illicit street drugs. They come in pills or powders. They are most often central nervous system stimulants containing varying amounts of over-the-counter preparations such as diet pills, decongestants, or caffeine. Most are sold as "speed." These have the effects of amphetamines. In large amounts they cause anxiety, rapid heartbeat, nausea, and difficulty breathing. In larger amounts they can cause seizures and even strokes. Act-alikes are manufactured to avoid state laws that prohibit look-alikes. They contain the same ingredients as look-alikes, but don't look like over-the-counter or prescription drugs.

LSD   (lysergic acid diethylamide), also known as acid, is a hallucinogen. The trade name is Delysid. It is a semisynthetic derivative of lysergic acid, found in ergot, morning glory seeds, and a fungus that grows on rye. LSD is a tasteless, odorless, colorless, crystalline solid sold in tablet, liquid, or capsule form. Ordinarily the liquid is dropped onto an absorbent pill or a small square of blotter paper, which is placed in the mouth. The drug then moves rapidly into the bloodstream. It is the most commonly used psychedelic drug, powerful because it first releases, then inhibits, natural substances in the brain.

The effects of LSD include imbalance, which is the first response after ingestion. Then the user experiences nausea, rapid pulse, enlarged pupils, and a rise in blood pressure. The "trip" lasts from four to fourteen hours, gradually tapering off.

The pleasantness of the experience depends on the user's frame of mind and surroundings. All five senses are heightened and time is distorted as the mind turns slowly inward. The senses can "cross over"—that is, music can be "seen," colors can be "heard." This phenomenon is known as synesthesia. If the user is unprepared and emotionally upset, a "bad trip" can occur. The drug has the power to unlock deeply repressed fears, anxieties, memories, and thoughts. Unfortunately, many people panic when the negative feelings occur and become psychotic. Some never come back to reality. Those who do may experience flashbacks during which their sensory perception is periodically disturbed without drug administration.

LSD is neither physically nor psychologically addictive, but it is extremely dangerous, because small quantities may cause hallucinations lasting for days. Withdrawal phenomena do not occur.

Marijuana is the dried herb *Cannabis sativa.* It is also known as pot, grass, or hash. The active ingredient is the chemical THC (tetrahydrocannabinol). The dried flakes of the plant look like oregano, and in the smokable form the "joint" resembles an unevenly packed cigarette. Marijuana can also be smoked in pipes or in water pipes (bongs), or concealed in hollowed-out cigars (blunts). The smoke has a sweet acrid odor that is easily recognized.

Mild use of the drug produces intoxication, pleasurable feelings of well-being, gaiety, and talkativeness followed by calm feelings of relaxation. But the drug affects different people in different ways. The immediate physical effects are a fast heartbeat and pulse rate, a dry mouth and throat, and bloodshot eyes. Mental effects include impaired short-term memory, altered sense of time, and reduced coordination. Therefore, this drug is particularly dangerous for drivers or anyone needing to concentrate or react quickly or accurately. In high doses its effects last from four to six hours and can include panic attacks or psychotic reactions. When used regularly for a long time, there is risk of psychological dependence, lack of motivation, and "burnout," during which the user becomes totally unaware of his surroundings but doesn't realize what is causing the problem. There is recent evidence that marijuana adversely affects the body's immune system. Dealers strengthen or lace the drug, so buyers are often unaware of the exact THC content of their purchase. So, contrary to what you may hear, marijuana is not a safe drug. Warning signs include red eyes and drowsiness. Users learn to disguise the effects by using eye washes. The unexplained appearance of Visine, for example, should alert a parent to the drug's use.

Meprobamate   is a minor tranquilizer. Trade names include Miltown and Equanil. These are white scored pills, used for muscle relaxation and as anxiolytics (anxiety relievers). They are less potent than the benzodiazepine-type minor tranquilizers such as Librium and Valium. They were the first minor tranquilizers before the benzodiazepines and were once very popular. Now they are not prescribed frequently.

Mescaline   (peyote) is a hallucinogen. It is also known as buttons, cactus, and mesq. Derived from the head (or button) of a small cactus native to northern Mexico and Texas, it belongs to the psychostimulant-hallucinogenic group of drugs and is chemically similar to adrenaline. Mescaline is less potent than LSD, and its effects include stimulation, alteration of perception, and hallucinations. It sometimes results in nausea and vomiting. These effects take place within two to three hours and last from four to twelve hours or more.

Mescaline is only a thousandth as potent as LSD; however, most purported mescaline samples are LSD. There is no physiological addiction reported, and tolerance develops very slowly. There does exist considerable cross-tolerance among LSD, mescaline, and psilocybin.

Methadone   is a fully synthetic narcotic-analgesic belonging to the opiate class of drugs. The trade name is Dolophine. It is also known as Dolly. Methadone is largely used in the maintenance treatment of heroin dependency because (1) it prevents heroin withdrawal symptoms; (2) it fulfills the addict's physical need for opiates; (3) at sufficiently high doses it blocks the effects of heroin through cross-tolerance so that a shot of street heroin during methadone treatment will probably give no significant additional effects; (4) it is a longer-acting drug than heroin, the average dose lasting twenty-four hours, making it more convenient to administer; (5) it is effective orally, breaking the reliance on the ritual of injection; and (6) it can be dispensed at treatment centers. Unfortunately, methadone has become a street drug itself, because addicts in treatment sometimes sell their supply. It is said to produce milder pleasurable sensations than heroin, but has the advantage of not causing severe withdrawal symptoms when doses are delayed. Some critics assert that methadone treatment merely substitutes one drug for another, but this view is not shared by the National Institute on Drug Abuse.

Methaqualone   is a nonbarbiturate sedative/hypnotic. It is a central nervous system depressant. It is no longer legally available. Trade names were Quaaludes, Sopor, Mequin, Parest, Optimil, and Somnifact. It is also known as ludes, sopors, 714s, and soap. It comes in tablet form. At low doses it produces feelings of sleepiness, well-being, and relaxation. At high doses it produces sleep, and was therefore once legally prescribed by physicians as a sleeping pill and tranquilizer.

There is a street myth that it increases sexual enjoyment, but actually it decreases sexual performance and the user becomes drowsy and "mellow."

Withdrawal can lead to convulsions, tremors, vomiting, and other serious symptoms. After prolonged usage, withdrawal requires medical supervision. Sometimes there is a parodoxical effect with jitters and hyperactivity, instead of sedation.

Overdose results in coma and eventually death. A Quaalude overdose should be treated as an emergency in the hospital, where life-support systems are available.

Mixing methaqualone with alcohol can cause a marked depression or an accidental overdose.

Morphine   is an opiate narcotic/analgesic. It affects the central nervous system by producing mental clouding, sleepiness, reduced ability to concentrate, general apathy, detachment from pain, and a feeling of "not caring." It is used medically to relieve major surgical or cancer pain, and to overcome diarrhea. It also reduces sex drive, hunger, and aggressive behaviors. Overdose produces coma, respiratory failure, and death.

Narcotics   are any drugs that dull the senses and produce sleep and/or a sense of well-being.

Nembutal.   See Barbiturates.

Nicotine   is a central nervous system stimulant. It is the active ingredient in cigarettes, cigars, and smokeless tobacco (snuff). It is made from the dried leaves of the plant *Nicotiana tabacum.* Its effects are complex and unpredictable. Users claim it calms the nerves. In new users, it is a stimulant. Long-term effects include heart disease, respiratory problems, and lung cancer. It also leads to psychological and physical dependence. Chances of getting lung cancer depend upon genetic predisposition, amount of tar per cigarette, depth of inhalation, number of cigarettes smoked each day, and number of years cigarettes have been used. Life span is reduced for the constant smoker, but people who smoke are physically incapacitated long before they die. Federal law requires cigarette packages to display warning messages.

Opiates   include opium and its derivatives, codeine, morphine, and heroin. Synthetic opiates include methadone meperidine (Demerol), oxycodone (Percodan), and propoxyphene (Darvon). Opiates in large doses cause stupefaction and even death.

Opium   is the source of opiate analgesics such as morphine and codeine. Traditionally, notably in China, it was smoked recreationally or ingested orally, but modern users prefer intravenous injection of more powerful pure opiates such as heroin or morphine. Medical use of raw opium has been virtually eliminated.

Overdose   describes the administration of a quantity of a drug larger than that normally or safely taken at one time or to which the system has acquired tolerance. Accidental overdoses often occur with the use of sedative drugs, opiates, barbiturates, and tranquilizers with or without alcohol.

Over-the-Counter Drugs   may be purchased without prescription. They are found on the shelves of all drugstores and even supermarkets. There are an estimated 350,000 OTC products with annual sales of four billion to five billion dollars. Some are subject to abuse, particularly certain cough remedies, sedatives, and painkillers. They contain potent analgesic/euphorogenic or hallucinogenic substances. It is possible to become dependent on them, so when you buy, read the labels and follow directions. And do not leave them within reach of youngsters.

Paraphernalia   is the assorted equipment and materials used to store or administer illicit drugs, or to make the drug high more intense. Some of the more widely used items are listed below by route of administration and drug:

- Smoking (marijuana, hashish, free-base cocaine, PCP, heroin, opium): paper envelopes or plastic bags, papers, rolling machines, pipes, strainers, bongs (water pipes or hookahs), containers (stash boxes), incense, fans
- Injecting (heroin, morphine, amphetamines, barbiturates): glassine envelopes or plastic bags, needles, syringes (can be modified eye droppers), tourniquets (belts, rubber hose, string), cotton wads

- Snorting (cocaine, heroin): glassine envelopes or plastic bags, razor blades and flat hard surfaces, such as mirrors (used to pulverize the drug into a fine powder), straws, rolled-up dollar bills, spoons, containers (usually small and often elaborate)
- Sniffing (glue, nail polish, gasoline, paint thinner, aerosol products, anesthetics, miscellaneous commercial products containing volatile solvents): paper bags, plastic bags, rags, balloons

PCP (phencyclidine hydrochloride) is a hallucinogen also known as angel dust or superweed. It was originally developed as an anesthetic and abandoned because of unacceptable side effects. It comes in powder, tablet, or capsule form and is easily made synthetically in garage or basement laboratories. Most often it is mixed with marijuana and cocaine and smoked. Unlike most hallucinogens, PCP exerts a depressant rather than a stimulant effect, but is often unpredictable and therefore does not fit clearly into any of the drug categories. In small doses its effects are memory gaps, general disorientation, and a feeling that one is outside oneself, watching what is happening. In larger doses its main dangers are related to impaired judgment and reduced sensitivity to pain. Prolonged use may damage the brain, producing behavioral problems that are manifested as emotional outbursts, tantrums, and violence. Its effects are felt minutes after injection and last for thirty to forty-five minutes. It can produce heart and lung failure and/or convulsions and permanent brain and nervous system damage. Withdrawal effects are not documented to date.

Polydrug Use   involves the use of more than one drug by the same person. Some users do not necessarily have a strong preference for any particular drug, while others are very specific in their choice of drugs.

Polydrug users often develop a "high" orientation and will take almost any drug or combination of drugs to experience the state of being high.

Proprietary (or brand-name) **Drugs** are drugs that are protected by patent against free competition as to name, product, composition, or process of manufacture (i.e., they "belong" to the manufacturer).

Psilocybin (Psilocin) is a hallucinogen also known as shrooms or magic mushrooms. Psilocybin is found in a number of Mexican mushrooms and is chemically related to LSD. It is usually taken orally, but is very expensive to synthesize or extract, so most of what passes on the street for psilocybin is actually LSD with or without PCP.

There is a rapid onset of effects after ingestion, which dissipate in three to four hours. It is not physiologically addicting. Therefore, withdrawal has not been observed or described.

Psychedelic Drugs are the hallucinogens; they are referred to as consciousness-expanding or mind-altering.

Psychoactive Substances are drugs that alter mood, perception, or consciousness.

Rohypnol is a powerful sedative that is banned in this country but legal in many other countries. Called "roachies," "roofies," and Mexican Valium among other names, it causes drowsiness in twenty to thirty minutes, and can cause coma and death. Dissolved in alcohol, it is used as a "date rape" drug, with the victim remembering nothing after the event.

Sedative/Hypnotic is a major classification of opioid and nonopioid sedative/hypnotic drugs. Examples of non-opioid members: methaqualone, chloral hydrate, barbiturates, glutethimide (Doriden), Noludar, methyprylon. Primary effects are calming, sedation, and induction of sleep. They are usually divided into four categories: barbiturates, alcohol, anti-anxiety tranquilizers, and nonbarbiturate sedative proprietary drugs.

All these drugs are dangerous when they are not taken at the recommended doses. They may cause both physical and psychological dependence. At high doses they may cause unconsciousness and death.

Stimulants   are a major classification of drugs that excite the central nervous system and produce an elevation of mood, a state of wakefulness, and increased mental activity and energy. They also suppress appetite. Stimulants are divided into two main categories: the primary stimulants, which act on the nervous system and include amphetamines and cocaine; and the secondary stimulants, which act primarily on the sympathetic nervous system and include nicotine and caffeine.

Users feel they have more energy, but these drugs also cause a racing heart and increased blood pressure and pulse rate. As the primary stimulant wears off in two to four hours, irritability and fatigue set in. Abusers eventually feel depressed. Teenagers often use these drugs with others such as alcohol and marijuana. Because of social pressure to be slim, many people use amphetamines to curb their appetites.

Overdose is serious and can cause muscle and chest pains and lead to convulsions, paralysis, and with high doses, coma and death. (See also Cocaine and Amphetamines.)

STP. See Designer Drugs.

Tolerance refers to the body's ability to adjust to the effects of a drug, requiring the user to take larger and larger doses to get the same effect. Tolerance occurs only when the drug is taken repeatedly. With LSD or heroin, for example, tolerance develops rapidly. With other drugs, such as alcohol, tolerance develops slowly.

Tranquilizers come in different strengths. The minor tranquilizers (anti-anxiety medications) are Xanax (alprazolam), Valium (diazepam), Librium (chlordiazepoxide), and Miltown or Equanil (meprobamate). The major tranquilizers (antipsychotic medications) are Thorazine (chlorpromazine), Mellaril (thioridazine), Stelazine (trifluoperazine), and Haldol (fluorobutyrophenone).

Effects of minor tranquilizers are loss of coordination, drowsiness, and general apathy. They act as muscle relaxants and anticonvulsants and also relieve anxiety. The major tranquilizers are used primarily to treat psychotic patients.

Withdrawal of the minor tranquilizers is the same as for barbiturates, but milder for some.

Tricyclic antidepressants are stimulants or "mood elevators." They include Tofranil (imipramine), Elavil (amitriptyline), Sinequan (doxepin), and Aventyl (nortriptyline). Initial effects of use include sedation, dry mouth, blurred vision, and constipation. Symptoms of withdrawal include nausea, headache, and general restlessness. Overdoses result in fever, elevated blood pressure, seizures, coma, and death. If CNS depressants (such as alcohol) are used in conjunction with any of these drugs, the sedative effects can be addictive.

This group of drugs is used for pharmacological treatment of depression. Nondepressed "control" subjects taking antidepressants become sleepy, poorly coordinated, and anxious. These drugs take two to three weeks to take effect; they are not commonly abused.

Withdrawal   refers to a cluster of characteristic reactions that occur upon abrupt cessation of a drug upon which the body has developed physical dependence and tolerance. It varies in intensity, depending upon the type and amount of drug used and the length of time the drug is used. Basically, it is a set of physiological symptoms, including sweating, shaking, convulsions, dizziness, and others, which are different for different drugs and different doses.

Withdrawal reactions can be fatal for some drugs. Prompt medical help can often prevent serious consequences.

Resources: Where to Get Information and Help

GENERAL INFORMATION

National Clearinghouse for Alcohol and Drug Information
 (NCADI)
P.O. Box 2345
Rockville, MD 20847-2345
1-800-729-6686
www.health.org

National Institute on Drug Abuse
NIDA Infofax
5600 Fishers Lane
Rockville, MD 20857
1-888-644-6432
www.nida.nih.gov

SELF-HELP

Alcoholics Anonymous—World Services
475 Riverside Drive
New York, NY 10115
212-870-3400
(AA is listed in most local telephone directories)

Al-Anon/Alateen Family Group Headquarters, Inc.
1600 Corporate Landing Parkway
Virginia Beach, VA 23454
1-800-344-2666

Families Anonymous
P.O. Box 3475
Culver City, CA 90231-3475
1-800-736-9805

Nar-Anon Family Group Headquarters, Inc.
P.O. Box 2562
Palos Verdes Peninsula, CA 90274-8562
310-547-5800
(Nar-Anon is listed in local telephone directories)

Toughlove
P.O. Box 1069
Doylestown, PA 18901
1-800-333-1069

FAMILY ACTION GROUPS

Community Anti-Drug Coalitions of America
901 North Pitt Street, Suite 300
Alexandria, VA 22314
1-800-542-2322

National Families in Action
2296 Henderson Mill Road
Suite 300
Atlanta, GA 30345
770-934-6364

MADD (Mothers Against Drunk Driving)
511 East John Carpenter Freeway
Suite 700
Irving, TX 75062
1-800-245-6233

National Parents' Resource Institute for Drug Education, Inc.
   (PRIDE)
3610 DeKalb Technology Parkway
Suite 105
Atlanta, GA 30340
770-458-9900

TREATMENT REFERRALS

NATIONAL DRUG AND ALCOHOL TREATMENT REFER-
RAL ROUTING SYSTEM: 1-800-662-HELP. Provides information on drug abuse and local health and treatment resources, and
also refers you to the National Clearinghouse for Alcohol and Drug
Information. If you hold on, you will be connected with a "special-
ist" to help you with your specific problem.

NATIONAL PARENTS' RESOURCE INSTITUTE FOR DRUG
EDUCATION, INC. (PRIDE): 770-458-9900 This is a not-for-
profit student helpline that will refer you to numbers in your local
area that can help.

SOURCES FOR CATALOGS ON DRUG AND ALCOHOL
USE AND ABUSE

American Council for Drug Education: 1-800-488-3784
Hazelden Publishing and Education: 1-800-328-9000
Johnson Institute: 1-800-231-5165
National Clearinghouse for Alcohol and Drug Information: 1-800-
729-6686

SUGGESTED READINGS

Joy Dryfoos, *Safe Passage: Making It Through Adolescence in a Risky Society: What Parents, Schools and Communities Can Do.* New York: Oxford University Press, 1998.

Neil Izenberg, *How to Raise Nonsmoking Kids.* New York: Byron Preiss Multimedia and Pocket Books, 1997.

C. Kuhn, S. Swartzwelder, and W. Wilson, *Buzzed: The Straight Dope About the Most Used and Abused Drugs from Alcohol to Ecstasy.* New York: W. W. Norton and Co., 1998.

Joanne Barbara Koch and Linda Freeman, *Good Parents for Hard Times.* New York: Fireside/Simon and Schuster, 1992.

Ruth Maxwell, *Kids, Alcohol and Drugs: A Parent's Guide.* New York: Ballantine Books, 1994.

Judith Seixas, *Alcohol: What It Is, What It Does.* New York: Greenwillow Books, 1979.

————, *Drugs: What They Are, What They Do.* New York: Greenwillow Books, 1987.

Judith Seixas and Geraldine Youcha, *Children of Alcoholism: A Survivor's Manual.* New York: HarperCollins, 1985.

U.S. Department of Education, *Growing Up Drug-Free: A Parent's Guide to Prevention.* Rockville, MD: National Clearinghouse for Alcohol and Drug Information, 1998.

U.S. Department of Health and Human Services, *Keeping Youth Drug-Free: A Guide for Parents, Grandparents, Elders, Mentors and Other Caregivers.* Rockville, MD: National Clearinghouse for Alcohol and Drug Information, 1996.

David J. Wilmes, *Parenting for Prevention.* Minneapolis: Johnson Institute, 1995.

Anthony E. Wolf, *Get Out of My Life, but First Could You Drive Me and Cheryl to the Mall?: A Parent's Guide to the New Teenager.* New York: The Noonday Press, Farrar Straus Giroux, 1991.

Index